The
Crocheter's
Quilt Book

THE
CROCHETER'S
QUILT BOOK

Afghans with Quilt Motifs
by
Elyse Sommer

Sedgewood® Press
New York

For Sedgewood® Press
Director: Elizabeth P. Rice
Associate Editor: Leslie Gilbert
Production Manager: Bill Rose

For Elyse Sommer, Inc.
Editorial Project Director: Elyse Sommer
Cover and Interior Design and Illustrations: Ann Jasperson
Photography: Bill Goldberg
Copy Editor: Gail Kahl
Sample Makers: Milly Beck, Lisa Cannon, Maria Giannitti, Susan Helige, Pearl
Hollander, Trudy Jaeggli, Elsie Jordan, Kathy Keller, Ruth Lichtenstein, Blanche
Miller, Hilda Sabbeth, Sophie Schwartz, Nina Smith, Shirley Strauss, Rose
Vartabedian.

Contents

Introduction

This book represents a marriage of two craft forms as compatible as the stars and stripes on the American flag, the patchwork quilt and the crocheted afghan. Both have endured through the centuries as pleasurable sources of warmth, decoration and creative self-expression. Both fill the modern crafts hobbyist's need for portable work methods that can produce something grand—the stuff of which an heirloom is made.

Who This Book Is For

Making afghans in authentic quilt patterns opens a window on an exciting new crochet experience. The patterns are interesting to crochet and beautiful to look at. What's more, they're loaded with possibilities for additional projects (the last project alone contains the makings of a dozen additional afghans).

For those of you who are new to crochet or consider yourselves in the novice class, let's get one thing straight, these projects are not for expert crocheters only! Nor will it take you a year and a day to complete an afghan. The emphasis on doing everything with simple, fast-moving stitches and in conveniently bite-sized squares or strips makes whatever you start blossom like a well-watered garden. To prove my point, some background about how the sample projects for this book were made:

I worked with a group of local crocheters with varying degrees of crochet proficiency and familiarity with quilting. My most expert *test pilots* were two yarn store owners, two women who were outstanding quilters as well as crocheters and one woman who had crocheted a very large afghan as well as a king-sized bed cover. The rest had more ordinary than extraordinary crochet experience. Practically all had full-time or part-time jobs or small children.

Each crocheter was given and met a four to eight-week deadline. As it turned out, most of the women finished much sooner and requested a second afghan to do. A few who had never made an afghan because they anticipated boredom from months and months of work, were thrilled to see how fast and enjoyably these designs moved along. For example, the woman who made the Broken Star (project #6, featured on the front cover) crocheted all the Diamond patches within two weeks and finished the Fill-In Squares and the border in four more days. Even the double layered Sunshine and Shadows (project #29) didn't go beyond the eight-week mark. I might add that it traveled on buses and a plane trip to Florida, arousing much curiosity and admiration along the way.

Now that we've settled the question of time and difficulty, a few words about methods and organization.

Our afghans are made with a cornucopia of sometimes complex-*looking* but always easy-to-crochet geometric motifs or patches which fall into four categories:

1. Patches crocheted in back-and-forth rows
2. Patches worked from the center out, like the familiar granny square
3. Three-Dimensional or Stuffed Patches
4. Patches worked according to a graph pattern.

Instructions for each patch are always followed by one or more projects in which the patch is used. Some projects are made with repeats of a single patch. Others combine several different patches. Both the individual patches and the overall patterns are designed to take full advantage of crochet's flexibility for building shapes and displaying its stitch personality in any direction.

The patches and projects are organized to build your crochet skill and pattern awareness in a logical sequence rather than in easy-to-harder progression. As it happens, the first three quilt afghans are probably ideal starter projects while the last, a roundup of everything you've learned, moves you towards working on your own with the patches and pattern blocks you've mastered.

Learn the Basics

Even though directions for individual projects are self-sufficient, *GENERAL INSTRUCTIONS* is a must reference section. It covers everything from basic stitches to quilt-specific stitches and techniques. So please, even if you're an experienced crocheter, be sure to check it out. Some techniques which may be new to you include the ways to arrange and join patchwork motifs, a special stitch I've dubbed the "quilt stitch," as well as instructions for making and attaching casings to transform your afghans into wall hangings.

Before You Begin

Here are a few suggestions to ensure success for your projects:
• Get out a ball of worsted weight yarn and an I or J hook and try out all the sample patches.
• Read through all the instructions. Review the pages with instructions for how to make each patch used. Check out anything which seems unfamiliar in *GENERAL INSTRUCTIONS.*
• Make a sample swatch to check if your gauge matches that given in the instructions.
• Take extra care to read through the *Notes* at the beginning of each project. These include instructions for enlarging or reducing patterns, as well as alternative color formats and working tips. The *Notes* are your key for perfect, personalized results.

While these afghans provide a new crochet experience, new does not mean difficult. As for the time involved, it varies. You can race through some projects in a week or two, or savor the experience over a month or more of spare time crocheting. In the long run it's not how long it takes you to finish that counts, but the pleasure that you derive from creating something practical and beautiful enough to occupy a place of honor in your home or the home of a friend or relative lucky enough to receive it as a gift.

General Instructions

If you're a beginner, this section will help you to gain altitude as a crocheter. If you're an experienced wielder of the crochet hook, you can soar through, only needing to stop wherever you see a new or different technique specific to our combination craft of quilting and crochet.

The Language of Crochet

Although crochet terms are spelled out in full in this section, directions for all projects are written in the shorthand commonly used for crochet instructions. Here is a list of abbreviations and symbols used, along with their meaning. Why not make a photocopy and use it as a bookmark.

beg	=	beginning	rnd(s) =	round(s)
ch(s)	=	chain(s)	sc =	single crochet
cont	=	continue	sk =	skip
dec(s)	=	decreas(es)	sl st =	slip stitch
dc	=	double crochet	st(s) =	stitch(es)
inc(s)	=	increas(es)	tog =	together
lp(s)	=	loop(s)	tr =	triple crochet
rep	=	repeat	yo =	yarn over hook

Special Symbols

× = times (as in repeat 2× instead of 2 times)
* = repeat directions from * as many more times as indicated.
() = read what's inside parentheses for explanatory comments or for instructions about how many times to repeat something.

Materials

Crochet requires just a few simple tools. Besides crochet hooks and yarn you need a measuring tape, a pair of scissors and a needle with a wide eye for weaving in loose ends and sewing patches together. For the stuffed projects use polyester batting which is available in most variety and sewing supplies stores. It's washable, light weight and can be cut to shape with a scissor.

Hooks

The old-time crocheter's work basket was apt to contain crochet hooks made out of ivory, bone, wood or vulcanite. Today, most hooks are made of aluminum or plastic and sized by letter or number. A wardrobe of hooks to serve all your needs would include a size K (for thicker yarns), sizes I and J (for worsted weight yarns), size G (for sport weight yarns).

You'll find the I hook most frequently specified for the afghans in this book. However, if you tend to work tightly, don't hesitate to switch to a J hook whenever an I size is given.

Yarns

Any worsted weight yarn—whether wool, synthetic, a blend or cotton, will work well for these projects. Sport weight yarn usually requires a stitch more per inch than knitting worsted. The lightness of the finished fabric compensates for the increased time needed to produce it. Thin yarns can of course be used double or even triple stranded, as can worsted weight yarns.

All projects list the yarn brand used to make the sample, with specifics about weight and fiber content. Color names listed are those used by the manufacturer. Whenever a manufacturer uses numbers instead of names, the number is parenthetically listed next to the generic color name. If you work with other yarns, use the yarn information in the Materials section as a guideline for estimating amounts and adjusting gauge. Whatever yarns you choose, it's best to stick to one weight for each project!

Yarn Prints

The multi-colored yarns available from many yarn companies provide an easy way to mimic the print patterns so popular in fabric quilts. The shades used for the "print" yarn are also available in solids. Thus you can coordinate a pink and blue print with solid pink and solid blue. You can also create your own "prints" by stranding two compatible shades together. If you do, remember to also double strand your yarn for any solid color design units.

Stitches

Slip Knot and Foundation Chain

All crochet begins with a slip knot and a chain from which you work straight up in rows or which you join into a circle so that you work in rounds. To make the beginning loop or slip knot:
• Hold the short end of the yarn in the left hand and bring the long end around to form a loop. Let the long end of the yarn form a vertical bar across the back of the loop and insert your hook underneath.
• Tighten the loop around your hook, but not too much. (*See GRANNY PATCHES AND PROJECTS* for how to start patches built from the center out with a loosened slip knot).
• To start the foundation chain, grasp hold of the slip knot with your left hand, bring the yarn over the front of the hook, and pull the yarn through the loop already on the hook.
• Continue to yarn over and pull the yarn through. To keep the chain from twisting, hold it between thumb and forefinger. Make as many chains as you need stitches per row or round *plus an extra chain.* This extra chain is known as the "turning chain" and counts as the first stitch of the first row or round of stitches.
• Count the stitches in your foundation chain, starting with the second chain, the one next to the loop holding the hook. *Do not count the slip knot.*

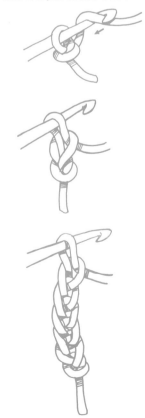

slip knot and foundation chain

Single Crochet

The single crochet stitch might well be called the universal stitch. All other stitches are variations designed to give more height, openness and surface texture. The geometric patterns that dominate our projects look best when worked with flat, dense stitches—to be specific, single crochet. To single crochet across the foundation chain:

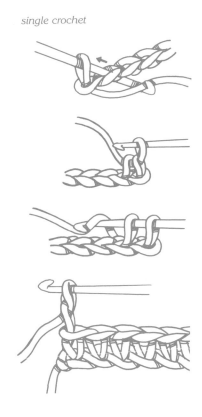

single crochet

• Insert your hook underneath the horizontal loops of the chain next to the hook (known as the second chain from the hook).
• Bring the yarn over the hook (yo) and pull through the chain loops on the hook so that 2 loops remain.
• Yarn over and pull through the remaining 2 loops and repeat across the row.
• When you get to the end of the row, chain 1 (ch 1) and turn. The chain 1 becomes the first stitch of the next row. Thus, "sc into each sc across" means to skip the chain 1 and begin single crocheting into the second stitch of the row. When you work in rounds you also begin with a single crochet into the first single crochet.
• To build your crochet fabric in this bottom to top direction, continue to work one row with the right side facing you and one with the wrong side facing you. *Remember to end each row with a chain 1 to turn around and begin the next row.*

Ridge Stitch

The ridge stitch provides the same crisp, solid look as the single crochet, plus surface texture. You may know the ridge stitch as a ribbed single crochet. Whatever you choose to call it, it's worked exactly like the single crochet except that you insert your hook into the *back top loop* instead of into both top loops.

Quilt Stitch

Many traditional afghan patterns call for the single crochet's taller cousins, the double and triple crochet (see Shell Edgings later in this chapter). While the height of these stitches makes the fabric grow rapidly, their openness does not provide the crispness that looks best with quilt patterns. As an alternative, there's an in-between sized stitch we'll refer to as the quilt stitch. It's a slightly taller and more open stitch than the single crochet and has a slant that looks particularly nice with the Stuffed Patch method developed especially for this book. Here's how to do it:

ridge stitch

• Begin as for a regular single crochet. Insert your hook through the space beneath the 2 top loops of a stitch, yarn over and pull through the space so that 2 loops remain on the hook. Yarn over and pull yarn through one of the 2 loops on the hook, then yarn over again and pull through the remaining 2 loops.
• Because this is a taller stitch, you need an extra turning stitch to step up to the next row or round. Therefore end each round with 2 chains (ch 2).

Slip Stitch

The slip stitch has no height, therefore it's a transitional not a pattern stitch. For afghans with quilt motifs it serves several vital functions:

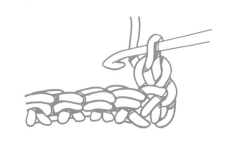

slip stitch

1. To end rounds in Granny and Stuffed Patches or borders. In crochet language this is known as "end rnd with sl st join." For projects worked in single crochet or ridge stitch with a chain one to "step up" from one row to the next the slip stitch join is always made into the first single crochet or ridge stitch, skipping the ch-1. (sl st in the first sc, or sl st in the first ridge st).

2. To get you from one place to another without breaking off yarn.

3. As a final border round to firm up the afghan's edges.

To form a slip stitch, insert your hook, yarn over and pull the yarn through the stitch and the loop on the hook, all in one motion.

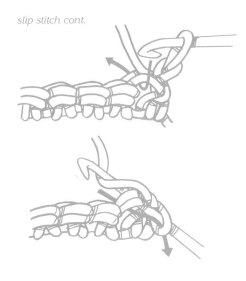

slip stitch cont.

Half Double Crochet Stitch

This is another transitional stitch. Because it's slightly taller than the single crochet stitch it's useful for straightening any dips or un-evenness that occasionally occurs when you create a design unit with different shapes (as during the progression from a circular to rectangular shape in project #26). To make it: Yarn over the hook, insert the hook through the 2 top loops and yarn through all 3 loops on the hook.

Bump Stitches

Traditional crochet pattern books are studded with stitches that accent flat surfaces with bumps or bobbles. While the emphasis in most patterns is on flat surfaces, there are occasions when bumps are appropriate. The bump stitch used throughout this book is one generally used as an edging, the picot. If you know and prefer an-other type of bump stitch, feel free to substitute it whenever a pat-tern calls for a picot stitch. To make a picot within a row or round:

• Insert hook as for a single crochet, chain 5, slip stitch back into the first chain (the 5th chain from the hook). Continue to single crochet until you want to make another picot, then repeat the chain 5 and slip stitch procedure.

• On the next row or round, crochet around the picot, holding it down with your forefinger to lock it in place.

To make a picot in a contrasting color: Attach the picot color yarn at the beginning of the row or round (carry it along and crochet around it at the back as explained in *Tapestry Stitch Color Changes*), complete the stitch before each picot with a yarn over in the picot color, and end the picot by slip stitching through the first chain in the background color.

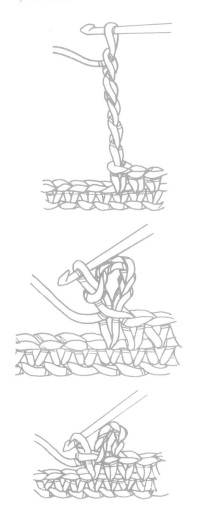

picot stitch

Crochet Techniques

Gauge

Gauge is your key for obtaining the proper size for your project. To test gauge, crochet a sample swatch. Lay it flat and use a ruler to measure how many stitches and rows occupy a one-inch or two-inch space. If you get more stitches per inch than the gauge speci-fied, switch to a larger size hook. If you get fewer stitches, try a smaller size hook. Unless your tension is extremely tight or loose, going up or down one or two sizes should do the trick.

For the projects in this book it's important to measure both hori-zontal and vertical dimensions of each design unit; also to measure squares or strips against each other so that they will line up prop-erly when you join them. This modular gauge is especially impor-tant if you plan to enlarge or reduce a project.

A word about the gauge given for the afghans. It was established to encourage a relaxed tension. This makes for a fast-building cro-chet fabric, without compromising the crisp look that's desirable.

Increasing and Decreasing

To increase, crochet two times into one stitch. Work increases at the beginning of rows into the second single crochet stitch and increases at the end into the next-to-the-last stitch. This method will give you the neat edge that's needed for joining patches.

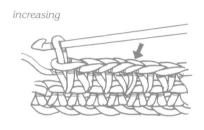

increasing

To decrease at the beginning of a row, work the first and second single crochet as follows: Begin the stitch, pull the yarn through 2 top loops, so that 2 loops remain on the hook. Insert your hook into the next stitch, yarn over and yarn through the 3 loops on the hook. To decrease at the end, decrease as above into the last two stitches. To decrease in the middle of a row (as for a Fill-In Triangle), skip a stitch.

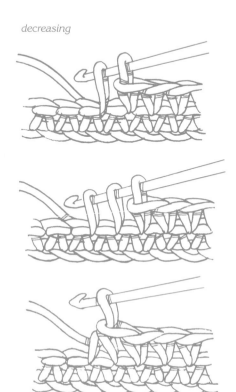

decreasing

Fastening Off

To fasten or end off:
• Cut the yarn, leaving a length of at least 6 inches, yarn over and pull through.
• Pull the end out, thread it through the eye of an embroidery or yarn needle and weave it in at the back of the work. Some crocheters knot the end of their yarn, but this is not necessary when you crochet around it in both directions as explained below.

Changing Colors at the End of Rows or Rounds

Changing colors is one of most exciting crochet techniques for capturing the charm and drama of fabric quilt patterns. The most familiar method for changing colors is to switch from one solid-color block to another, as in a striped pattern. Such color changes are made at the end of a row or round as follows:
• Crochet to the last stitch of the row or round.
• Work the last stitch until you have 2 loops left, cut the yarn as you would to fasten off, tie on the new color yarn.
• Complete the last yarn over in the new color. You can either weave in the ends later with a tapestry needle, or crochet them in at the back. Crocheting the ends in is faster and avoids having a lot of finishing tasks pile up. Here's a weaving-in method that will secure the yarn ends to withstand wear and washings: Leave an end long enough to crochet around it for several inches in both directions. Begin weaving in the ends on one row, then continue the process on the next row.

Tapestry Stitch Color Changes

Still more interesting effects and an extra-rich texture are possible when you alternate colors within a row or round. This is called Tapestry Stitch or Color-through-Color. The idea is to carry along the colors for a particular design unit, so that each can be picked up as needed. It can be a bother to juggle many colors. However, limited to 2 colors, as all our Tapestry Stitch patches and projects are, it's ultra-simple. Here's how it works:
• Start the tapestry pattern with the front or right side of the work toward you (if you work your color changes right, there should be little if any visible distinction between the front and the back). Hold the color you'll be switching *to* on top of the row and crochet around it as you work.

• Complete the last yarn over of the stitch before the color switch in the color to which you're switching.
• If you're changing colors once per row or round (as in Row-by-Row Patches Six and Seven), leave the yarn you're not using hanging at the back and continue crocheting with the new yarn. When you need the dropped yarn again on the returning row (when the wrong side is toward you), switch colors as you did before. If you're switching twice in one row or round (as in Row-by-Row Patches Five and Eight), carry the yarn you're not using along and crochet around it. To work with color charts, see *Graph Pattern Projects.*

To Prevent Tapestry Stitch Color Show-Through

A slight glimmer of the carried-along color is nothing to get excited about. To keep show-through to a minimum, give a gentle tug to the carried-along yarn before you switch colors. For absolutely no show-through, try this Stretch-in-the-Back method:
• Begin your color change as for the "regular" tapestry stitch technique.
• When you switch colors on the return row (wrong side toward you), *do not carry and crochet in the yarn not in use.* Instead, drop and leave it hanging. When you need it again, *gently and loosely* stretch it across the back to complete the stitch you're switching from (you yarn through in the stretched-across color). The yarn will be attached at each end.
• On the next row (right side toward you) switch colors as usual, but crochet around two layers of yarn, the yarn you're carrying and the yarn attached at the back. To repeat, you do not crochet in the carried color when the wrong side is toward you. You crochet around a double layer when the right side is toward you.

Joining Patchwork Motifs

Joining the shapes into pattern or design blocks and then sewing these blocks together is known as Patchwork or Piecing. Crochet provides several techniques for attaching the pieces within a block and then joining the blocks into an overall pattern.

Hand Sewing

This produces a smooth, flat join. To sew-join:
• Pin the patches together with the right sides together.
• Thread a blunt yarn needle with matching color yarn. Secure the yarn with a knot and join by catching the top loop of each matching pair of stitches. When finished secure the yarn by going two or three times into the edge stitches.

Weaving Patches Together

This produces a virtually seamless finish. Here's how to do it:
• Lay your patches face up, with the edges touching, but not overlapping.
• Thread an embroidery needle with matching yarn.
• Weave through the centers of the loops at each edge.

Zig-Zag Machine Joining

If you have a sewing machine that does zig-zag stitches, by all means consider using it to join your pattern pieces. Zig-Zag joins work best with smooth, non-fuzzy yarns. To machine join put your

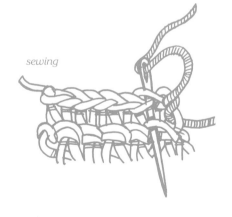

sewing

weaving

quilt face down underneath the presser foot and use thread that matches the main color.

Crochet Joining Finished Patches

You can crochet as well as sew finished design units together. For a slip stitch join with a ridge on the back, pin your patches together with the right sides facing each other, tie a knot on the end of your yarn and pull it through the top loops of the stitches at each edge. For a join that produces a decorative ridge on the surface, pin the patches with the wrong sides facing in and single crochet through the top loops at each edge.

Crochet Joining As You Work

One of the nicest things about crochet is that it allows you to let a pattern grow as you work. Many of our afghan pattern blocks are made from several design patches with each new patch crocheted directly to the top or side edge of the previous one. When you join one patchwork motif to the top edge of another you simply switch from one color and stitch pattern to another. While side edges don't have the same smooth finish as the top and bottom of a piece of crochet, you can nevertheless crochet join lengthwise and crosswise patches as you work. To do so, insert your hook into the spaces between rows exactly as you would for a regular row of stitches.

One thing you should bear in mind is that a lengthwise patch crocheted to a long side edge is likely to produce a slightly different gauge than what you get when you crochet crosswise. A good rule of thumb to avoid rippling or pulling is to skip one stitch every 4 inches. In other words, if you were working in a gauge of 7 stitches per 2 inches crosswise, crochet 13 stitches every 4 inches lengthwise.

Pattern "Sets" and Size Adjustments

Arranging Patterns or "Setting the Pattern"

"Setting" a pattern refers to the way you arrange your design units to build the overall pattern. You can use a straightforward plan whereby square pattern units are set together. This is the straight set and the simplest. And it always gives pleasing results.

Another very effective arrangement is to set a square on its point. Such Diagonal Sets look more complex than Straight Sets but they're often even faster and easier to assemble, especially with the help of the Fill-In Triangle (see Row-by-Row Patch Two). If you want to change a straight set pattern to one with the pattern blocks set on the diagonal, use the chart in this section to help you figure out how many patches to make.

Enlarging or Reducing Patterns

Patterns crocheted in modular units are not only conveniently portable but also easier to enlarge or reduce. You either make more or fewer units or you increase or decrease the pattern block dimensions. To estimate the effect of unit size changes on the afghan's overall dimension:

• Measure the edges of individual straight set units, then multiply by the number of units per row. Example: If you increase ten-inch squares to twelve-inch squares an afghan with four squares across

and six squares down is enlarged from forty by sixty inches to forty-eight by seventy-two inches.
• Measure diagonal set units from point-to-point and multiply that measurement by the number of units per row. Example: A six-inch square in a diagonal set pattern takes up eight and a half inches vertically and horizontally. Therefore, an afghan with five units across and five units down measures 42½ by 42½ inches. If you add one unit across and two units down, your overall width is increased by eight inches and overall length by sixteen inches (51 by 59½ inches).

Finishing Methods

Surface Crochet

This is less a stitch than a method for running raised lines on top of a finished crochet surface. These lines can be vertical or horizontal, straight or curved, slip stitched or single crocheted. Surface Crochet, like applique work in fabric quilting, is a useful accent technique. Try doing it on top of a piece of crochet, as follows:
• Outline the direction of your Surface Crochet line with straight pins.
• Put a slip knot on a hook a size smaller than the one used to crochet the background piece.
• Hold the hook on top of the crochet (right side of work), insert it into a hole in the fabric, bring the hook back to the top and make your stitch.
• Continue as needed, making an extra stitch or two for a sharp turn and going around a curve (see the handles in project #32) without extra stitches.
• When finished, thread the yarn ends into a wide-eyed needle and weave in at the back to secure.

Corded Edges

While a final round or row of slip stitches will serve to firm up your afghan's edges, there's nothing quite like a Corded Edge, especially in a contrasting color. This is a single crochet stitch in reverse. Here's how to do it: Starting at the left side, with the right side toward you, chain 1, insert the hook in the next stitch *to the right,* bring the yarn through underneath the top loops and yarn through as for a single crochet stitch.

Shell Edgings

Another very pretty edging is made with a shell pattern which combines the single crochet stitch with one or both of its taller cousins, the double and triple crochet stitch. One very attractive shell edging occupies five stitches and works as follows: Attach yarn in any single crochet, skip 2 stitches, double crochet 5 times into the next stitch, skip 2 stitches and repeat (sk 2 sts, *5 dc in next st, sk 2 sts, rep from *). Project #33 uses a single-double-triple crochet stitch pattern. For readers unfamiliar with these tall stitches, here's how you make them:

To double crochet, yarn over, insert your hook underneath the 2 top loops, yarn through 2 loops; next yarn over and through 2 loops to complete the stitch. To make a triple crochet, yarn over twice. Pull the yarn through 2 loops, yarn over and pull through 2 loops twice more to complete the stitch.

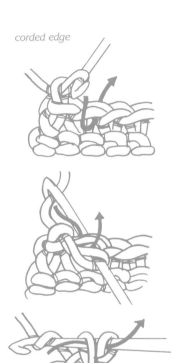

corded edge

shell edging

Borders

Most afghans don't need more than a simple frame. Such frames can be crocheted around individual pattern units—what quilters call Lattices—or around the entire afghan. The easiest method for making a border is to crochet it directly to the edges as described in Crochet Joining As You Work. The three most commonly used borders are All-Around Borders, Strip Borders and Strip & Square Borders. Before we detail how these are made, a tip: For a smooth transition from the pattern edges to the border, single crochet one row or round (wrong side toward you) in the yarn to match the border stitches.

All-Around Border

Here you crochet around the pieced motifs, using the side, top and bottom edges as a foundation round. You increase at the corners to keep them nice and sharp. To do so, either go 3 times into the corner stitches (3 sts into each corner st) or, if your yarn is on the stretchy side, go 2 times into the stitches before and after the corners (2 sts into each st before and after corner st). End the round with a slip stitch into the first single crochet or ridge stitch (skip the chain one), then chain one to step up to the next round.

To start the next round you can keep going around without turning or turn and go back around. The first method, referred to throughout these pages as the Up-and-Around method, is the one many of you are probably familiar with. The second method, referred to as the Chain-and-Turn method, is less familiar but extremely valuable for afghans with quilt motifs. Individual project directions give the method considered best for that particular afghan. However, as the two methods can usually be used interchangeably, instructions for both are included here for easy reference.

With the Chain-and-Turn method, you crochet into the edge stitches. Adjust the gauge used for the main pattern so that you have approximately 1 stitch less for every 4 inches (this is a rule of thumb formula). Increase at the corners on alternate rounds only. Like the border gauge, corner increases are subject to adjustments. If the border pulls, increase more often.

With the Up-and-Around method, you crochet into each edge stitch and increase at the corners on each round. If the border pulls, switch to a size larger hook.

While it is recommended that you sacrifice portability and crochet your border directly to the edges, you could work each side of a border separately and join when finished. To do so, chain a foundation to match the dimension of the edge to which it will be attached. Work in back and forth rows over the foundation, increasing at the beginning and end of every other row so that your corners will be mitered.

Strip Borders

These begin with the top and bottom edges. The side portions reach from end to end of the top and bottom border pieces. Like All-Around Borders, Strip Borders are best crocheted directly to the edges.

Strip and Square Borders

Here the border pieces match the dimensions of each edge and a contrast colored square fills in the corner spaces. This is a particularly lovely and quilt-like border, and, as you'll see when you get to project #8, very easy and enjoyable to make.

Finishing and Maintenance

Blocking

Most projects will benefit from a light steam pressing or blocking once all the patches are joined. Blocking can correct any surface unevenness or differences in patch dimensions. However, if overdone, blocking can also give your design surface a flat, lifeless look. The best time to block is before you join the design units. To start the blocking process, lay your work face down on an ironing board or other flat surface. Place a dampened cloth on top of the crochet surface then bring your hot iron down lightly. You'll hear a hissing sound. *Do not press down as you would to iron a handkerchief or blouse.* After everything is assembled, lay the finished afghan on a mattress or carpet (again, right side down) and, *without touching the fabric,* move your steam iron over the joined seams.

Casings for Hanging Afghans

You can drape your afghan across a bed, sofa or chair, snuggle up with one when you watch tv, or wrap it around a baby. In a room that doesn't get heavy foot traffic, you can even use it as a rug, ideally over carpeting which prevents slipping. You can also hang your handiwork on the wall.

Afghans that work best as wall hangings are either stuffed or made with non-stretchy, sturdy yarn. To keep your hanging from sagging or getting stretched out of shape, you need a top and bottom casing (approximately ½ inch in diameter) and 2 rods. To make and attach casings:
• With yarn to match the afghan edges, chain 9 (approximately).
• Single crochet in each ch. Ch 1 and turn.
• Single crochet in each sc and slip stitch into the first single crochet to form a circle. Chain 2.
• Double crochet in each single crochet (see Shell Edgings for how to double crochet), end the round with a slip stitch into the first double crochet. Chain 2 and continue around until the tube reaches from edge to edge across the top.
• Fasten off and sew in place at the back, about an inch below the top.
• Make another casing and attach at the bottom.
• Insert rods through the casings.
• To prevent your hanging from stretching, bolster the bottom rod with a few unobtrusively placed nails.

Caring For Afghans

Like all fine handmade items, your afghans should be treated with care and respect. Let the kids sit on them, but with their shoes off. Air them regularly and keep them away from exposure to direct sunlight. And, if you put them in storage during the summer, wash them or have them cleaned first.

To machine wash (synthetics only): Turn to the cold water cycle and use a mild detergent. To prevent "pilling" put your afghan into a large mesh bag, with the wrong side out. Put on the "air" or lowest cycle of your drier or spread on a clean blanket to dry.

To wash by hand (wool, cotton or synthetics): Fill your bathtub with cold water and gentle detergent and swish around. Rinse with cold water and lay on large towels or a sheet blanket to dry.

Row-by-Row Patches

and

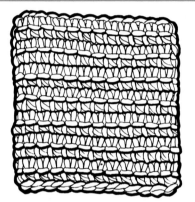

Projects

In this first group of
patches and projects, you
crochet back and forth
over a foundation chain.
It's as simple as making a
potholder but, with the
right combination of
shape, color and piecing,
you end up with a true
heirloom.

Row-by-Row Patch One/Plain Patch

Plain Patches are any squares or rectangles crocheted in bottom to top progression, in solid colors or stripes. You could make a whole houseful of afghans strictly with Plain Patches. They're also stunning when used in combination with other quilt motifs, as in projects #8 and 15. Fabric quilters call such arrangements Alternate Plain Blocks.

Applications: Projects # 1, 2, 3, 4, 5, 8, 9, 11, 15.

To Make Sample Patch
Ch 9 (8 plus 1 to turn).
Row 1: Sc into 2nd ch from hook, sc in next 7 chs (8 sts). Ch 1 (the ch-1 counts as the first st of the next row), turn.
Row 2: Sc into each sc across (8 sts). Ch 1, turn.
Rows 3–8: Rep rows 1 and 2 (right side toward you on all odd-numbered rows; wrong side toward you on all even-numbered rows).

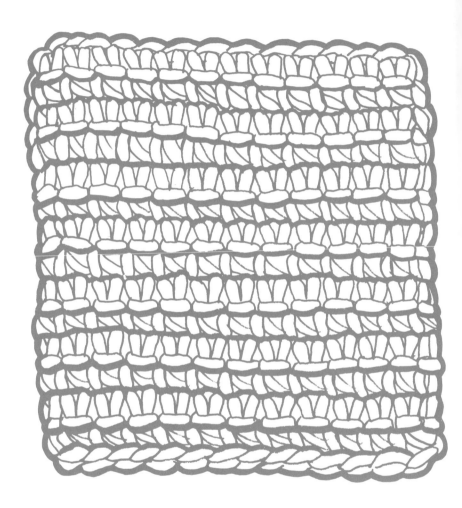

Arranging Plain Patches

You can arrange Plain Patches so that the stitches face all in one direction or into a vertical-horizontal pattern. Let's add a lengthwise patch to the first one using the method of crochet joining described in *GENERAL INSTRUCTIONS—Joining Patches.*

Row 1: Turn the first patch sideways, work a sc into each of 8 edge sts. Ch 1, turn (the edge is the equivalent of the foundation chain).

Row 2: Sc into each sc across (8 sts).

Rows 3–8: Rep rows 1 and 2.

Remember

• Count your stitches and rows regularly.

• Measure finished patches against each other to make sure they'll line up evenly when joined.

• Think of a row of stitches crocheted into a side edge as if it were a regular row. And bear in mind that crocheting into a long side edge will produce a slightly fuller gauge than the horizontally worked piece. The rule of thumb for adjusting such differences is to reduce the main pattern gauge by one stitch every four inches when you use a long edge as your foundation.

#1 Striped Geometric

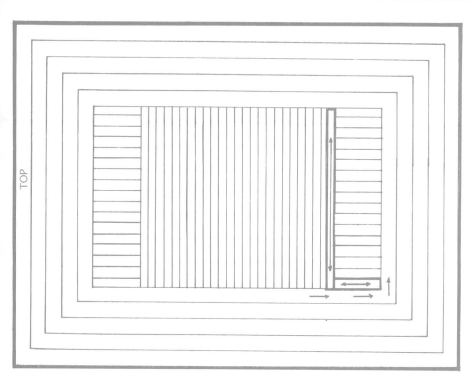

This interpretation of an early twentieth century crib quilt is handsome enough to fit into a simple or sophisticated room setting. It's made with just three Plain Patches but the secret is in the vertical-horizontal placement and the striped frame which pulls everything together. Don't be surprised if everyone in your family asks for one in his or her own favorite color combination.

Patches Used: Plain Patches.

Materials/Measurements
Finished Size: Approx. 45 by 63 inches.
Yarn: Coats & Clark Red Heart "Preference" (4 ply orlon, 3½-oz.), 8 dark gold, 6 eggshell.
Hook: Size I.
Gauge: 7 sts = 2 inches, 7 rows = 2 inches.
Short Plain Patches = 6 by 28 inches.
Long Plain Patches = 28 by 34 inches.

Notes
• To enlarge the pattern, add 2 stripes and 6 stitches per row to the short and long sections. To enlarge further, add additional pairs of stripes and extra stitches.

• Any number of colors can be used as a contrast for the eggshell stripes. You could also stick with the gold stripe and substitute blue, green or pink for eggshell, OR use light and dark shades of one color.

• Come back to this pattern when you learn to make Stuffed Pouch Strips (see *STUFFED PATCHES AND PROJECTS*). The stripes would divide nicely into a grid for this type of double-layered crocheting.

Directions
Short Plain Patch
Make 2
With gold, ch 22.
Row 1: 21 sc. Ch 1, turn now and throughout.
Rows 2–6: 21 ridge sts (switch colors at end of 6th row by finishing last yo in eggshell).
Row 7: 21 ridge sts.
Rows 8–13: 21 sc (switch back to gold at the end of 13th row). Rep rows 1–13 st and color pattern until you have 17 stripes, starting and ending with gold.
A Word to the Wise. Stop to measure your first stripe. Add or subtract stitches or switch to a hook which will give you the specified dimension.

Center Plain Patch

Make 1

With eggshell, ch 96 (if you've added or subtracted sts for the short strip, adjust the number of sts accordingly). Work same st and color pattern as for the short patch for 21 stripes (beg and end with eggshell).

A Word to the Wise. Stop after a couple of rows and make sure that the width of the center patch and the edge of the short stripe patch both line up. If the center patch is either too narrow or too wide, go back and adjust stitch base.

To Make Border

Sew or crochet join the striped patches as shown in the assembly diagram. Then work a 5-stripe border as follows:

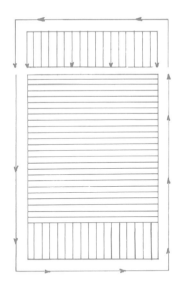

Round 1: (Right side toward you, beg at any corner) with eggshell, sc into edge sts all around (dec gauge to 13 sts per 4 inches), join with a sl st in the first sc. Ch 1, turn now and throughout.

Round 2: (Wrong side toward you) Sc into every sc (2 sc in sc before and after corner sc).

Rounds 3 and 5: Sc into each sc around (do not inc at corners).

Rounds 4 and 6: Rep rnd 2 (switch to gold at end of rnd 6).

A Word to the Wise. If corners seem too tight, increase at corners on every round.

Round 7: With gold, ridge st in each sc.

Rounds 8 and 10: Ridge st in each st (2 sts in sts before and after each corner st).

Rounds 9 and 11: Ridge st in each st (do not inc at corners).

Round 12: Ridge st in each st (2 sts in sts before and after corner sts—switch to eggshell).

Round 13: With eggshell, ridge st into each ridge st.

Rounds 14 and 16: Rep rnd 2.

Rounds 15 and 17: Rep rnds 3 and 5.

Round 18: Rep rnd 2 (switch to gold).

Round 19: Rep rnd 7.

Rounds 20 and 22: Rep rnds 8 and 10.

Rounds 21 and 23: Rep rnds 9 and 11.

Round 24: Rep rnd 12 (switch to eggshell).

Round 25: Rep rnd 13.

Rounds 26 and 28: Rep rnd 2.

Round 27 and 29: Rep rnds 3 and 5.

Round 30: Rep rnd 2 (do not switch colors).

Round 31: (Optional) sc all around from left to right for Corded Edge finish (see *GENERAL INSTRUCTIONS*). Fasten off.

Finishing

• Tie on eggshell yarn at any edge of the center section.

• Surface Crochet all around the center section to create a raised line between the striped patches and the border.

• End Surface Crochet rnd with a sl st join and bring yarn to wrong side to weave in as detailed in *GENERAL INSTRUCTIONS—Surface Crochet.*

#2 Amish Split Bars

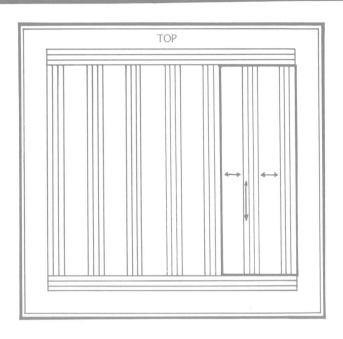

TOP

Amish quilters have a reputation for coaxing excitement out of the simplest geometric motifs. Their striped patterns, called Bars, give dramatic proof that this reputation is well deserved. When you alternate solid and narrowly striped Bars you get what's known as a Split Bar pattern. Our crocheted Bar pattern mixes solid-color and striped bars. For added surface interest, the Bars are arranged horizontally and vertically. Patches Used: Plain Patches.

Materials/Measurements
Finished Size: Approx. 52 by 57 inches.
Yarn: Charity Hill Farm hand-spun wool (knitting worsted weight, 3½-oz.) 5 light sheep, 3 each rust heather, denim blue heather, green heather.
Hook: Size I.
Gauge: 7 sts = 2 inches, 7 rows = 2 inches.
Solid-color patches = 4 by 44 inches.

Notes
• For a more rectangular shape, lengthen the horizontally worked single crochet strips (light sheep) and add the necessary additional stitches for the split bars (denim blue and rust heather stripes).
• To emphasize the Amish influence, substitute the border instructions from project #22, using rust heather for the Fill-In Square.
• For a more intense color scheme, switch to deeper hues of the illustrated colors—tan for the horizontally worked strip, electric blue and bright crimson rust for the stripes, and kelly green for the border. For a complete color switch, substitute deep purple or blue for light sheep and use black and brown or navy for the stripes. Yet another way to obtain a different effect is to use the same color for the horizontally worked strip and the center stripe of the vertical split bar.

Directions
Horizontal Strips
Make 6
With light sheep, ch 15.
Row 1: Sc into the 2nd ch from the hook and in each ch across. Ch 1, turn (14 sts).
Row 2: Sc into each sc across. Ch 1, turn.
Rows 3–154: Rep row 2.
A Word to the Wise. Stop after an inch to make sure your strip has the right dimension. Once you finish the first strip, don't bother counting rows for the other five. Instead, use the first strip as a yardstick.

To Add the Vertical Stripes
Make 6

1. Crochet 1 set of stripes to the side edge of 5 horizontally worked patch strips; crochet 2 sets of stripes to each side edge of the remaining horizontally worked patch strip. Work each stripe as follows:

Row 1: (Right side toward you) With denim blue heather, sc into the sts along the side edge of the horizontally worked strip in a gauge decreased to 13 sts for every 4 inches. Ch 1, turn now and throughout.
A Word to the Wise. Check the suggested gauge for the vertical stripe before you go any further. If the horizontally worked strip is longer than it was before, redo the first blue denim heather row with fewer stitches. If it's shorter, start over with more stitches.
Row 2: (Wrong Side toward you) ridge st in each sc.
Row 3: Ridge st in each ridge st.
Rows 4–12: Rep row 3 (switch to rust heather at end of row 4, switch back to blue denim heather at the end of row 8). Fasten off.

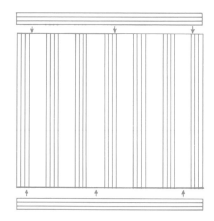

2. Join the combined horizontal-vertical patches as shown in the assembly diagram (join the 5 patches with the stripes at one edge first, then add the patch with stripes at each edge).

Top and Bottom Striped Patches
Make 2

Row 1: With rust heather (start at top right edge), sc into the edge sts along the top of the joined patches (work in same gauge as for the stripes). Ch 1, turn now and throughout.
Rows 2–4: Sc in each sc across (switch to denim blue heather at end of 4th row).
Rows 5–8: Ridge st in each sc across (switch to rust heather at end of 8th row).
Rows 9–12: Sc in each sc. Fasten off. Rep rows 1–12 at other end of afghan.

To Make Border

Round 1: With green heather (start at any corner, right side toward you), sc into the edge sts all around (use same gauge as for vertical stripes). End rnd with sl st join to first sc. Ch 1, turn now and throughout.
A Word to the Wise. Lay work flat before you continue. Adjust stitch gauge if anything ripples or pulls.
Round 2: Sc into each sc around (2 sc into sc before and after each corner sc).
Rounds 3, 5, 7, 9, 11: Sc into each sc around (do not inc at corners).
Rounds 2, 4, 6, 8, 10, 12: Rep rnd 2 (if corners pull, inc at corners on every rnd or as needed).
Round 13: (Optional) with denim blue heather, sc one rnd from left to right for Corded Edge as detailed in *GENERAL INSTRUCTIONS* (3 sc into each corner sc).

#3 Split Rail

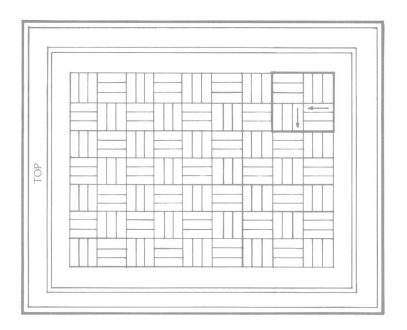

Crochet a Plain Patch in three stripes and you've got a rather ordinary piece of crochet fabric. But watch what happens when you repeat one color in a pair of striped patches, and arrange them so that the twice-used color runs through everything like a railroad track. Our Split Rail pattern has the center stripe in each patch ridge stitched for extra surface interest. This pattern is also known as Rail Fences and Railroad Tracks.

Patches Used: Plain Patches

Materials/Measurements
Finished Size: Approx. 54 by 66 inches.
Yarn: Talon American (4 ply Dawn Sayelle knitting worsted 3½-oz.) 6 each copper and dark gold, 7 each grape and scarlet, 17 fisherman white (4 white, 1 grape, 1 scarlet for border).
Hook: Size I.
Gauge: 7 sts = 2 inches, 7 rows = 2 inches.
Plain patches = 6 inches square.
Special Abbreviations:
Patch A = copper/gold/white stripes.
Patch B = grape/scarlet/white stripes.

Notes
• To create your own split rail color combinations, pick two compatible dark colors for each patch, plus a light color for the connecting rail. To illustrate, a pale green or blue could connect medium blue/red and dark green/gold stripes.
• If you'd like to explore this pattern for another and different looking afghan, check out the *STUFFED PATCHES AND PROJECTS* section.

Directions
The Plain Patches
Make 31 Patch A, 32 Patch B
Ch 22 (copper for Patch A, grape for Patch B).
Row 1: Sc into the 2nd ch from the hook and each ch across. Ch 1, turn now and throughout (21 sts).
Row 2: Sc in each sc across.
Rows 3–7: Rep row 2 (switch to gold or grape at end of row 7).
Row 8: Ridge st in each sc across.
Row 9: Ridge st in each st across.
Rows 10–16: Rep row 9 (ridge st row 16 in white).
Row 17: Sc in each ridge st across.
Rows 18–22: Sc in each sc across. Fasten off.

To Join the Patches

• Follow the assembly diagram to join patches a row at a time—a patch with stitches turned lengthwise alternating with one with the stitches going crosswise to make a parquet pattern.

• When all patches are joined in rows, join row 1 to row 2, 3 to rows 1–2 and so forth.

A Word to the Wise. You can save time by joining pairs of patches as you work. To be specific: When you finish one patch, single crochet into its side edge to begin a second patch.

Optional Finishing Step

With white, Surface Crochet along the edges of all the white rails.

To Make Border

Round 1: With scarlet (start at any corner with right side toward you), sc into the edge sts in a gauge to give you 13 sts for every 4 inches. End rnd with a sl st join to the first sc. Ch 1, turn now and throughout.

Round 2: (Wrong side toward you on this and all even-numbered rnds) sc into each sc (2 sc into the sc before and after each corner—switch to white).

A Word to the Wise. Stop to make sure that the suggested border gauge will keep your work flat. Increase number of stitches if border pulls, decrease if it ripples.

Rounds 3–24: Rep rnds 1 and 2 in white (switch to grape at the end of rnd 10, switch back to white at the end of rnd 13, switch to scarlet at the end of rnd 22).

A Word to the Wise. If border seems tight, increase at the corners on each round or as needed.

Row-by-Row Patch Two/Fill-In and Corner Triangles

It's no exaggeration to call these two patches indispensable. They turn problem spaces into opportunities for adding stitch interest without any sewing. Best of all, they're easy and fun to work. Because these are accessory modules, you'll find them used throughout the book.

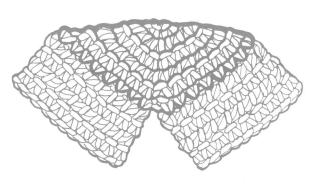

To Make Sample Corner Triangle
Position 2 Plain Patches on the diagonal from point to point.
Row 1: Sc in each of 9 edge sts of one square, from the bottom to the midpoint. Ch 1, turn.
Row 2: Work a dec into the first 2 sc (see *GENERAL INSTRUCTIONS—Increasing and Decreasing*), sc in each sc across row until 2 sts remain, dec in last 2 sc. Ch 1, turn.
Rows 3–5: Rep row 2 until 1 st is left. Fasten off. Note: If you decrease triangles more gradually, they will be taller and thinner, as in project #18.

To Make Sample Fill-In Triangles
Use the Corner Triangle sample to work the Fill-In Triangle in between the diagonally set Plain Patches.
Row 1: 15 sc into two adjoining edges—7 sc down along one edge (from B to C in illustration), sk 1 at the inside corner, 8 sc up along the adjoining square's edge (from C to D in illustration). Ch 1, turn now and throughout.
Row 2: 13 sc across, 1 dec (see *GENERAL INSTRUCTIONS—Increasing and Decreasing*) at the beg, middle (the inside corner) and end on this and all rows to follow—7 sc (from D to C in illus), sk 1, 5 sc (from C to B).
Row 3: 10 sc (6 from B to C, 4 from C to D).
Row 4: 7 sc (5 from D to C, 2 from C to B).
Row 5: 4 sc (3 from B to C, 1 from C to D).
Row 6: 1 sc from the ch 1 directly into last st. Fasten off.

To Work Triangles Without Breaking Off Yarn
You can move from Corner Triangle to Fill-In Square and from one Fill-In Square to another in an uninterrupted flow as if you were crocheting a regular row. Here's how:
1. When you finish the first Corner Triangle, work 8 sl sts into the edge from the triangle's point to its base (X to B in illustration).
2. *Sc the Fill-In Triangle, sl st from its end (Y in the illustration) to the beg of the next Fill-In, rep from * for as many Fill-Ins as needed. Finish with a final Corner Triangle.

#4

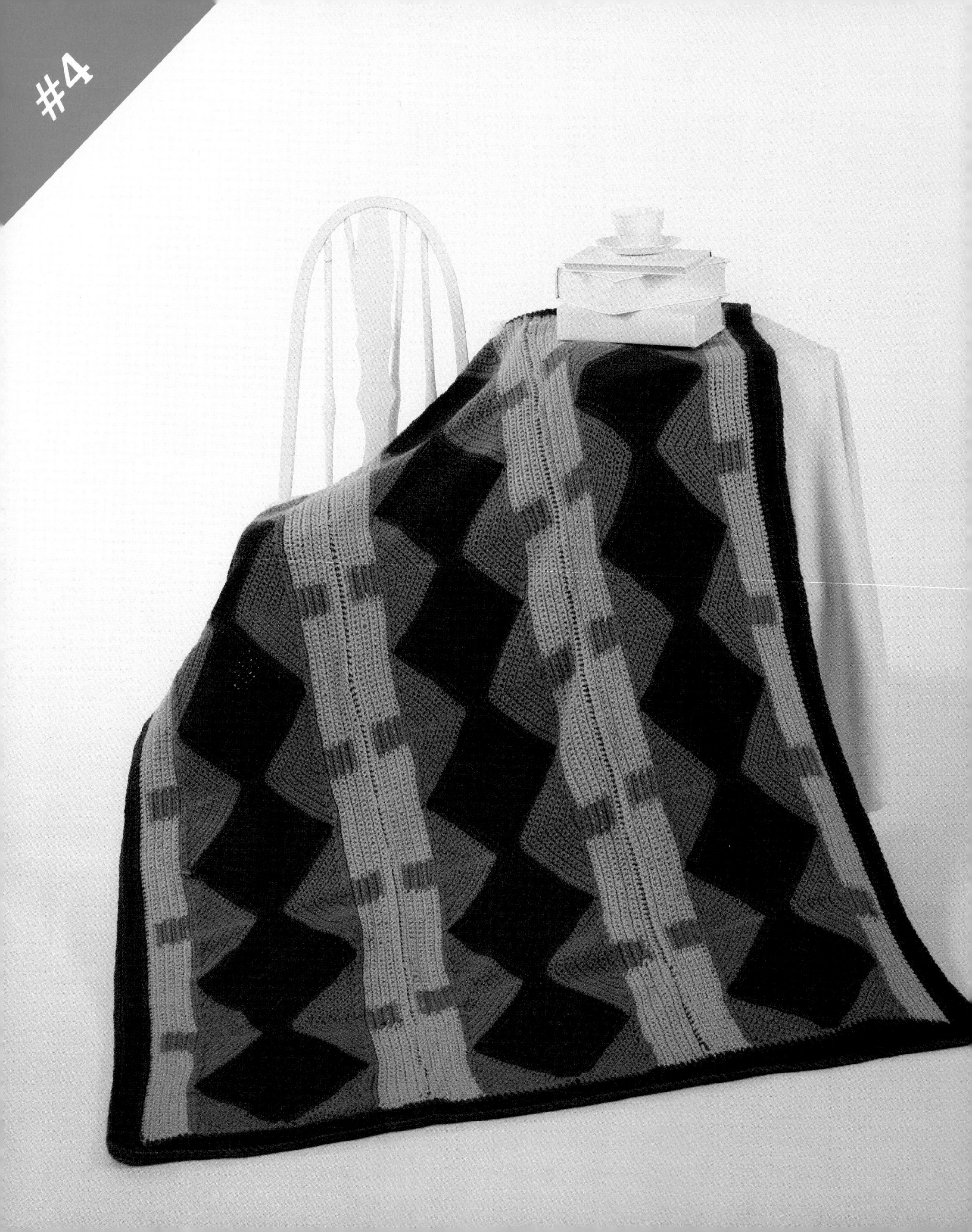

#4 Diamonds and Arrows

These handsome diamond square strips are made with Plain Patches set on the diagonal with Fill-In and Corner Triangles to even out each side. Additional Plain Patch strips that introduce the Tapestry Stitch technique transform the Fill-In Triangles into arrows.
Patches Used: Plain Patch Squares, Corner and Fill-In Triangles

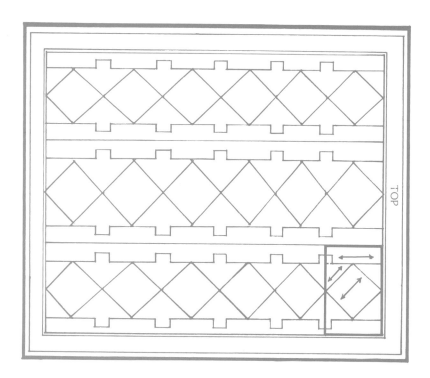

Materials/Measurements
Finished Size: Approx. 46 by 60 inches.
Yarn: Nevada Grand Prix Woolton (wool knitting worsted, 1.7-oz.) 8 each dark red (#574) and beige (#568), 6 light blue (#572), 3 dark grey (#632).
Hook: Size I.
Gauge: 7 sts = 2 inches, 7 rows = 2 inches.
Each Plain Patch = 6 inches square.

Notes
• This is an ideal design for getting the hang of crocheting fill-ins continuously, without breaking the yarn as detailed in the previous section.
• Lengthen the afghan by adding diamond squares to each strip. Widen it by making additional strips.
• If you're making this afghan for a baby, substitute a pale pink with dark pink edging for the diamond squares, and use two shades of blue for the fill-in sections. Denim blue diamonds with purple edging, and green and gold for the fill-in areas would be good choices for an older child's room.

Directions
Diamond Square Strips
Make 3
1. With red, ch 22 then work 21 sc across, ch 1 and turn for 21 rows. Fasten off and rep 17 times.
2. Position squares so the points touch. Pick up a square and with grey, work *21 sc into one edge and 21 sc in the next, pick up another square. Rep from *5 × (you'll have a 6-patch strip). Ch 1, turn and work 1 ridge st into each sc (3 ridge sts into the sts at the points, sk a st at the inside corner). Fasten off.
3. Rep step 2 at the other side of the 6-patch strip.

To Fill In Spaces and Corners

Make 2 Corner and 5 Fill-In Triangles for each side of one strip
1. Turn the strip sideways so that the bottom patch is to your right. With light blue, sc a Corner Triangle to the first edge of first square—from the bottom point to the midpoint (beg with 21 sc into the edge then dec at beg and end of each row until 1 st is left).
2. Sc another Corner Triangle to the last edge of the square at the other end of the strip—from its mid point to its top corner.
3. Sc 5 light blue Fill-In Triangles into the spaces between adjoining diamond squares. Beg each Fill-In Triangle with 18 sc into one edge (down toward the inside corner), 18 sc into the edge of the adjoining square (from the corner to the next point).
A Word to the Wise. Remember to make 1 decrease at the beginning, middle and end of each row.

The Tapestry Stitch Arrow Patches

Crochet join 1 to both sides of each strip as follows:
Row 1: With beige, (strip turned sideways with right side toward you), 13 sc into the top edge of the first Corner Triangle, 11 sc into the first part of the first Fill-In Triangle, switch to light blue for 6 sc (carry and crochet around beige at the back). Cont across row with *23 sc in beige, 6 sc in blue, rep from * 3 ×. Switch back to beige and cont with 23 sc into edge of second Corner Triangle. Ch 1, turn now and throughout.
A Word to the Wise. Begin color changes on the stitch before you work with the new color. For example, in the row above, you complete the 23rd beige stitch in light blue and the 6th light blue stitch in beige.
Row 2: In the same color pattern as first row, sc in each sc across (carry yarn not in use along the top and crochet around it, or use Stretch-In-Back technique described in *GENERAL INSTRUCTIONS—Tapestry Stitch Color Changes*).
Rows 3, 5 and 7: Rep row 1.
Rows 4 and 6: Rep row 2 (switch to beige on last yo).
Rows 8 and 9: With beige, sc in each sc across row. Fasten off.
Rep rows 1–9 at other side of strip.

To Join and Border

1. Place two finished pattern strips together with right sides facing out. Crochet join with grey.
2. Crochet join third strip to the pieced strips.
3. (Right side toward you) With grey and hook a size larger, sc into edge sts all around (3 sc into corner). End rnd with sl st join to first sc.
4. Ridge st in each sc (3 sc into each corner sc). Ch 1.
5. Ridge st in each ridge st (3 sts into each corner st). Ch 1 and rep for 10 rnds (rnds 5 and 6 in red, rnds 7 to 10 in grey). Fasten off.

A Word to the Wise. Lay work flat after you complete first border round. If border pulls, go back and increase the number of stitches into each edge. If border ripples, switch back to smaller size hook.

Row-by-Row Patch Three/Fill-In Squares

The Fill-In Square is a first cousin to the Fill-In Triangle as it's also used to fill in open spaces. The point of the square is pushed out by skipping 2 stitches in the middle of each row. Like the Fill-In Triangle, this patch looks particularly handsome in ridge stitch. Applications: Projects #5, 6, 9, 14 and 35 (squares 14 and 15).

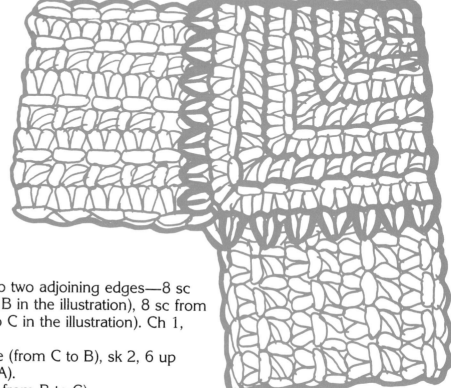

To Make Sample Patch
To make your sample patch you'll need two Plain Patches (8 sts per row, 8 rows each), positioned so that the squares touch at the points.

Row 1: With Color B, work 16 sc into two adjoining edges—8 sc down along the first edge (from A to B in the illustration), 8 sc up along the second edge (from B to C in the illustration). Ch 1, turn now and throughout.
Row 2: 14 sc—8 along the first edge (from C to B), sk 2, 6 up along the adjoining edge (from B to A).
Row 3: 12 sc (5 from A to B, sk 2 7 from B to C).
Row 4: 10 sc (6 from C to B, sk 2, 4 from B to A).
Row 5: 8 sc (3 from A to B, sk 2, 5 from B to C).
Row 6: 6 sc (4 from C to B, sk 2, 2 from B to A).
Row 7: 4 sc (1 from A to B, sk 2, 3 from B to C).
Row 8: 2 sc (1 from B to C, sk 2, 2 from C to A).
Row 9: 1 sc into the last stitch. Fasten off.

#5 Trip Around the World

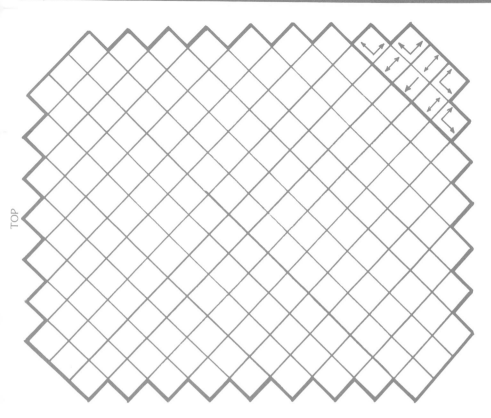

TOP

This pattern gets its name from the way bands of color travel around one or more color blocks at the center. It's all done with strips of Plain Patch squares in carefully arranged, paired colors. The three teal center squares in our crib-sized crochet adaptation are repeated with ridge stitched Fill-In Squares. Quilters refer to these jagged borders as Prairie Points. Patches Used: Plain Patches, Fill-In Squares.

Materials/Measurements
Finished Size: Approx. 38 by 47 inches.
Yarn: Scheepjeswol Superwash Zermatt (wool worsted, 2¾-oz) 6 each lavender (#4840) and teal (#4838), 5 each fuchsia (#4878) and purple (#4872), 4 red (#4885).
Hook: Size I.
Gauge: 10 sts = 3 inches, 10 rows = 3 inches.
Plain patch and fill-in squares = 3 inches square.

Notes
• If you prefer a straight to an irregular edge, substitute Fill-In Triangles for the Fill-In Squares.
• For a bigger afghan, enlarge the size of the patches by 1 inch or add additional color segments to each strip (either two or three additional shades or repeats of the colors already used).
• The rich, deep tones shown here echo the colors fabric quilters used in the mid-19th century when this pattern first became popular. For a 1920s–1930s look (another period when many Trip quilts were made), try a pastel palette— peach, light and deep pink, gold, moss green and sky blue.

• Compare this pattern to another concentric square pattern, project #28. Once you master the Stuffed Square-Into-Strip, you may want to make a second Trip Around the World afghan using that technique.

Directions

1. With lavender, sc 2 Plain Patches (10 sts each row, 10 rows).

2. Follow color and assembly chart to sc 15 strips. Work the Plain Patches within the strips as per step 1, but with the first row of each new color block in ridge st. Make 2 strips each with 3 color blocks, 2 with 5, 2 with 7, 2 with 9, 2 with 11, 2 with 13 and 3 with 15.

3. Lay out finished Plain Patch strips to match assembly diagram and join a row at a time.

A Word to the Wise. It's a good idea to begin piecing with the longest strips.

4. With teal, ridge st 7 Fill-In Squares into the spaces between the end color blocks at the top and bottom of the pieced afghan and 9 Fill-In Squares into the spaces at each side. (Beg each fill-in with 11 sts into the edge of the first square and 11 into the adjoining edge).

5. With teal, work one sc into each st all around (sk 1 st at the inside corners, work 3 sc into each point st). End rnd with sl st join. Fasten off.

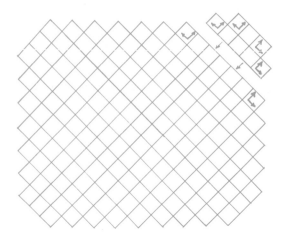

Row-by-Row Patch Four/Diamond

Combine two triangles into one unit and you've got a diamond. You increase a stitch at the beginning of each row for the first half of the patch, then decrease a stitch at the beginning of each row for the second half. It's as simple as that. Applications: Projects #6 and 7.

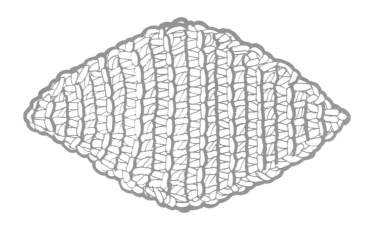

To Make Sample Patch

Ch 3.

Row 1: 1 sc into 2nd ch from hook and next ch. Ch 1, turn now and throughout.

Row 2: 1 sc in each of 2 sc across.

Row 3: 1 sc in first sc, 2 sc into next sc.

Row 4: 1 sc in first sc, 2 sc into next sc, 1 sc in next sc.

Rows 5–8: Cont to work 1 sc into first sc, 2 sc into the next sc (inc here instead of into first sc makes for smoother joining edge), 1 sc in each sc to the end of the row (see *GENERAL INSTRUCTIONS— Increasing and Decreasing*).

Row 9: 1 sc into the first sc and each of the next 8 sc, sc the last 2 sc as one (1 dec made).

Rows 10–14: Rep row 9.

Rows 15–16: 1 sc in each of 2 sc. End Diamond with ch 1, turn and sl st into 2nd sc.

#6 Broken Star

This exuberant and bold design, also known as Carpenter's Wheel and Dutch Rose, dates to the late nineteenth century. If our crochet adaptation looks complicated to you, relax. You'll be positively amazed at how quickly and easily the Star grows and the bright yellow background squares fall into place.

Patches Used: Diamonds, Fill-In Squares, Fill-In Triangles.

Directions

1. Sc 16 blue and 16 red Diamonds (46 rows each—1 inc at the beg of rows 3–23 and 1 dec at the end of 24–44).

2. Position 8 Diamonds (alternate red and blue) to form Star pattern. Join at the lower half of each Diamond.

3. With yellow, sc 8 Fill-In Squares between the upper halves of the Diamonds. Beg the fill-ins with 23 sc into edge of one Diamond (from top point to corner), and 23 sc (from corner to top of adjoining diamond).

A Word to the Wise. Lay your work flat after the first two Fill-In Squares. If there's any rippling, go back and reduce the number of stitches. If the square isn't full enough, add a stitch or two along each edge.

Materials/Measurements

Finished Size: Approx. 52 by 52 inches.

Yarn: Scheepjeswol Superwash Zermatt (wool worsted, 1 ¾-oz) 7 each red (#4885) and blue (#4838), 5 yellow (#4880).

Hook: Size I.

Gauge: 7 sts = 2 inches, 4 rows = 1 inch.

Diamonds = 11½ inches from point to point.

Notes

• To enlarge the afghan, make larger Diamonds. If you do, be sure to also increase the number of stitches for the Fill-In Triangles.

• If you want your stars to pop out from the background, work all the Fill-In Triangles and Squares in ridge stitch.

• For another dazzling color combination, consider orange and gold Diamonds against a bright red background. For a more subdued flavor, rust and leaf green on a beige background would be nice.

4. Arrange 3 Diamonds so that you have 1 blue sandwiched between 2 red. Sew join at the lower half of each Diamond. Rep 3 ×.
5. Rep step 4 but this time sandwich 1 red Diamond between 2 blue ones.
6. Sew join the 3-diamond units into the spaces between the Fill-In Squares, alternating the colors.
7. With yellow, sc 2 Fill-In Squares (with same number of sts as previously made squares) in the spaces between the 2 sets of Diamonds at each corner (8 more Fill-ins).
8. Sc another Fill-In Square into the spaces between the Fill-In Squares just made (4 more Fill-Ins).
9. Sc a Fill-In Triangle into the remaining spaces between Diamonds (2 at each side—beg each with 23 sts into each of 2 adjoining edges).
A Word to the Wise. Remember that you decrease 2 sts on each Fill-In Square Row (by skipping 2 stitches in the middle) and that you decrease 3 sts on each Fill-In Triangle Row (1 each at the beginning, middle and end).

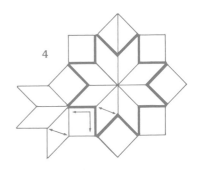

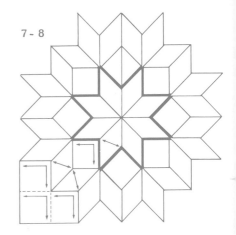

To Make Border
Round 1: With blue (beg at any corner, with right side toward you) sc into the edges all around (dec your gauge to 13 sc for every four inches). End rnd with sl st join to the first sc. Ch 1, turn.
A Word to the Wise. Lay work flat and adjust stitch gauge if anything ripples or pulls.
Round 2: (Wrong side toward you) sc into each sc around (2 sc into each sc before and after corner sc), sl st in first sc. Ch 1, turn.
Rounds 3–12: Rep rnds 1 and 2 (switch to red at end of rnd 4 and back to blue at the end of rnd 8).
A Word to the Wise. If corners seem tight, increase at corners of each round.
Round 13: (optional) 1 sl st into each sc all around.
Fasten off.

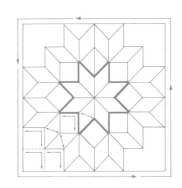

#7 Baby Blocks

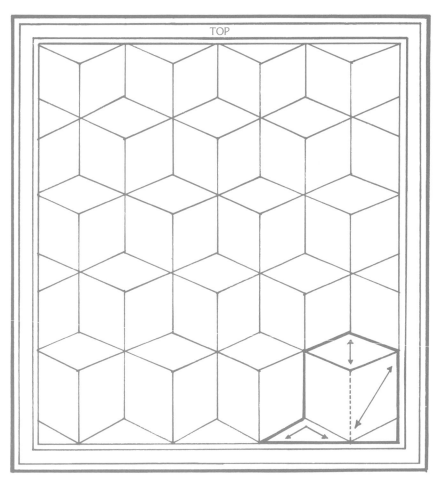

TOP

Old-time Baby Block quilts are intricate mosaics, pieced with hundreds of tiny Diamonds which create the illusion of rows filled with three-dimensional blocks. Happily, crochet allows you to obtain the same effect with larger, easier-to-join pieces. Like so many much-made and much-loved patterns, this one has acquired a string of name tags throughout the years, the best known being Tumbling Blocks, Stair Steps and Illusion. Patches Used: Diamonds, Corner and Fill-in Triangles.

Directions
1. Sc 58 Diamonds—12 each oyster white and beige, 8 each light misty blue and camel, 7 each dark oxford grey and denim blue, 4 light oxford grey (48 rows with 1 inc at the beg of rows 3–24 and 1 dec at end of rows 25–46).
2. Sc 2 half-Diamonds in denim blue and 2 in light oxford grey (stop after row 24).
3. Arrange the finished Diamonds into 3-patch Baby Blocks (1 Diamond for the top and 2 for the sides), then assemble into the following color sequence (*the rows with asterisks beg and end with half Diamonds*):

Materials/Measurements
Finished Size: Approx. 51 by 69 inches.
Yarn: Bernat Sesame "4" Heathers (wool knitting worsted, 3½-oz.) 3 each oyster white and beige; 2 each misty blue, denim blue, camel, dark oxford grey, light oxford grey; 1 claret.
Hook: Size I.
Gauge: 7 sts = 2 inches, 9 rows = 2 inches.
Diamond Patch = 12 inches from point to point.

Notes
• Because the Diamond patches must line up exactly, it's important to check for any differences in gauge from yarn shade to yarn shade. Adjust such size discrepancies by single crocheting once around any patches that are smaller than the rest (1 sc into each sc—3 sc in each of the 4 corner sts).
• For a super simple alternative color scheme, use the same color blocks throughout. This is most effective with a trio of strong colors; for example, a deep lavender lid, with indigo blue and dark purple sides.

	BOX TOP	LEFT SIDE	RIGHT SIDE
Row One	Oyster White	Denim Blue	Misty Blue
*Row Two	Dark Oxford Grey	Oyster White	Light Oxford Grey
Row Three	Misty Blue	Camel	Beige
*Row Four	Denim Blue	Dark Oxford Grey	Beige
Row Five	Oyster White	Beige	Camel

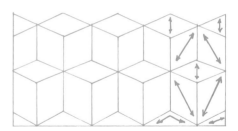

4. Join the Baby Blocks a row at a time, starting with the top row (from right to left). To join, ∗ place a Diamond "box top" and a Diamond side unit tog with the right sides facing out. With a size smaller hook and yarn to match the "box top", sc through both edges (from the top to the midpoint), pick up second side unit and join to other half of "box top" Diamond. Rep from ∗ for the other Baby Blocks in the row (you'll have a strip of Baby Blocks with open seams between each of the side diamonds).
5. Sew join the open seams between the side Diamond units.
6. Rep the steps 4 and 5 procedure for 4 more rows of Baby Blocks. On rows 2 and 4, beg by joining a Diamond to a half-Diamond "box top" (from the half-Diamond's center to its point) and end with a Diamond joined to another half-Diamond (from its point to its center).
7. Line up baby block rows 1 and 2. With dark oxford grey, and the right sides facing out, sc through both edges across the row (sk 1 at the inside corners where the Diamond points meet and work 3 sc in the sc at the mid point of the "box top" patch.
8. Join the top of row 3 to the bottom of row 2 in misty blue, the top of row 4 to the bottom of row 3 in denim blue and the top of row 5 to the bottom of row 4 in oyster white.

To Finish and Border
1. With claret, sc 4 Fill-In Triangles into the spaces between the Diamonds at the top and bottom of the pieced afghan and 1 Corner Triangle to the edges at each corner (beg the Corner Triangles with 21 sts into the edge and the Fill-In Triangles with 21 sts into each of two adjoining edges).
A Word to the Wise. Remember, you can crochet Corner and Fill-In Triangles as you would a continuous row. For a refresher on how to do this, see the instructions for Row-by-Row Patch Two.
2. With claret and a hook one size larger (start at any corner, right side toward you), sc into the edges all around (3 sc in each corner sc). Ch 1. Cont for 11 more rnds (2 claret, 6 light oxford grey, 3 claret). Fasten off.
3. Add a line of Surface Crochet along the edge of each Diamond across the top, working 3 sts into the points and skipping a st at the corners where the diamonds adjoin. (This compensates for the fact that the "tops" do not have a joining ridge.)

Row-by-Row Patch Five/Checkerboard Grid

Checkerboard Grids can be divided into any number of color blocks. The design squares thus created are named according to the number of color blocks—Four-Patch, Eight-Patch, Nine-Patch and so forth. Our sample patch and the projects that follow focus on the Nine-Patch which is probably the best known of these Checkerboard Grid squares.

Applications: Projects #8, 9, 32 (border), 35 (squares 4 and 18).

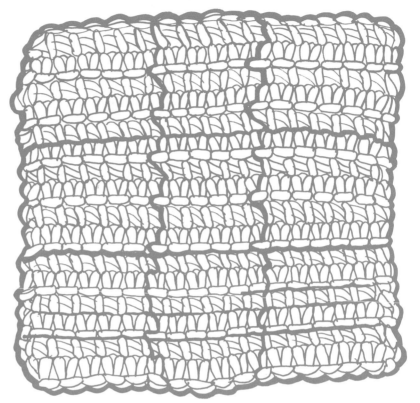

To Make Sample Patch
Ch 22 (7 Color A, 7 Color B, 8 Color A). Ch 1, turn.
Note: To work the foundation in the Checkerboard pattern, finish the 7th ch with a Color B yo, work around the Color A yarn when you use Color B, finish the 7th Color B yo with Color A and leave it hanging in place when you work with Color A. Switching colors on the foundation chain makes for a seamless connection between pattern squares. This is especially important when they're set right next to each other as in project #9. For patterns like project #8 you could make your foundation chain all in the main color.

Row 1: Sc into the 2nd ch from the hook and each ch across (7 in Color A, 7 in Color B, 7 in Color A). Ch 1, turn.
Row 2: In same pattern as row 1, sc into each sc across. Ch 1, turn.
Rows 3–7: Rep row 2.
Rows 8–14: Rep row 2 in B-A-B color pattern.
Rows 15–22: Rep row 2 (A-B-A color pattern). Fasten off.

Remember
• When switching colors, always finish the last yo in the next color.
• Carry along and crochet around any color you'll be using again in the same row. And give a gentle tug to the carried color before you switch back to it.
• Re-read the instructions for the Stretch-In-Back tapestry stitch technique described in *GENERAL INSTRUCTIONS.*

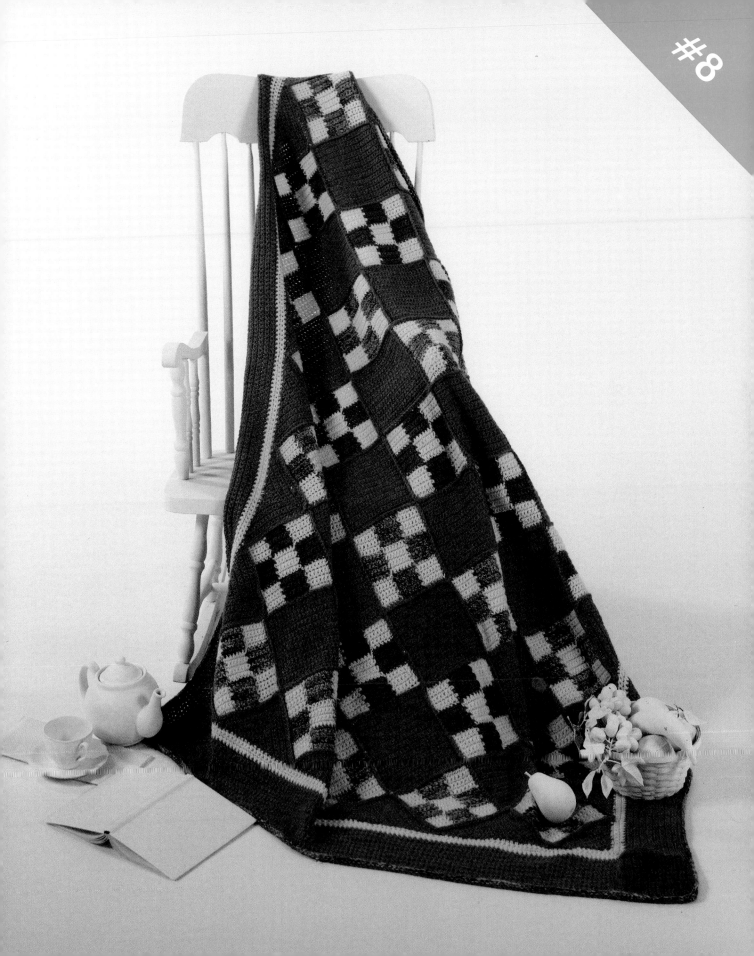

#8 Nine-Patch

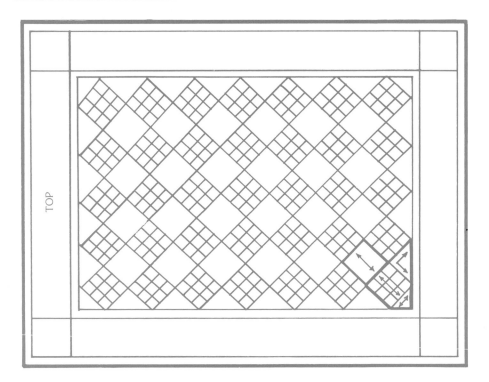

Quilts with Nine-Patch blocks have been a staple in American women's hope chests since the early 1800s. Our crocheted Nine-Patch alternates Checkerboards in two different color combinations with a solid-color Plain Patch. The squares are worked in strips for smooth and easy piecing. A border worked partially in rounds and partially in rows, adds the perfect finishing touch.
Patches Used: Checkerboard Grids, Fill-In and Corner Triangles, Fill-In Squares.

Directions
1. Sc two #1 patches, following the instructions for the Checkerboard Grid sample in the previous section (beg with a foundation ch of 8 white, 8 blue, 9 white—24 sts each row, 8 rows each set of color blocks).
2. Sc two 3-patch strips (#1-#3-#2).
3. Sc two 5 patch strips (#1-#3-#2-#3-#1).
4. Sc two 7-patch strips (#1-#3-#2-#3-#1-#3-#2).
5. Sc three 9-patch strips (2 strips with patches in #1-#3-#2-#3-#1-#3-#2-#3-#1 sequence, 1 strip in #2-#3-#1-#3-#2-#3-#1-#3-#2 sequence).

Materials/Measurements
Finished Size: Approx. 52 by 68 inches.
Yarn: Bernat "Berella" (4 ply acrylic knitting worsted, 3½-oz.) 13 copper heather, 6 white, 5 denim blue tweed, 4 blue heather.
Hook: Size I.
Gauge: 4 sts = 1 inch, 4 rows = 1 inch.
Each patch = 6 inches square.
Special Abbreviations: #1 patch = blue denim tweed/white Checkerboard.
#2 patch = heather blue/white Checkerboard.
#3 patch = copper heather Plain Patch.

Notes
• Be sure to make a sample of both patches used and measure them against each other for any discrepancy in gauge. This can be caused by a slight difference in one yarn shade or in your tension from one type of patch to the next. Whatever the cause, it's easily adjusted by adding or subtracting a stitch or row from one of the patches.
• To harmonize the Nine-Patch with your room decor, crochet the Plain Patches in a yarn shade to match the dominant room color. Pick colors for the Checkerboard patches to match curtains, rugs and accent items.

6. Join the strips into 9 rows as in assembly diagram. It's best to join the 9-patch strips first (sandwich the strip that begins and ends with #2 patches between the strips that begin and end with #1 patches), then add the shorter strips at each side.

7. Join the individually made #1 patches h to the middle square of each 3-patch strip.

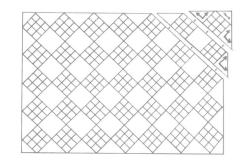

To Fill In the Spaces Between the Edge Patches

1. With copper heather, sc 4 Corner Triangles to each of 4 #1 patches at the corner of the afghan (beg triangles with 25 sc into the edge).

2. With copper heather, sc 4 Fill-In Triangles into the spaces at the top and bottom and 6 into the spaces at each side (beg the fill-ins with 25 sc in the edge of one square and 25 sc in the edge of the adjoining square).

To Add Surface Crochet Ridge (optional)

This is a decorative touch, worked with copper heather along the inside edges of the fill-in units and around the Plain Patches.

1. Surface Crochet along the base of the Corner Triangle at the lower right, up along the inside edges of the Fill-In Triangles and the base of the Corner Triangle at the top.

2. Rep step 1 at the other side of the pieced afghan (this time beg at the top left and work down to the lower left Corner Triangle base).

3. *Surface Crochet along one inside edge of a Fill-In Triangle (you're working from the top to the bottom, a vertical row of Plain Patches at a time), cont along the edges of the next 6 Plain Patches and one edge of the Fill-In Triangle at the bottom. Rep from * 7 × until all copper heather patches are framed with Surface Crochet.

To Make Border

1. With copper heather (beg at the top right edge with the wrong side toward you), sc into edge sts all around (dec gauge to 7 sts for every 2 inches). End rnd with a sl st join to first sc (switch to white). Ch 1, turn.

2. With white, *sc into each sc around, sl st in first sc. Ch 1, turn. Rep from * for 3 more rnds (3 sc in each corner sc on second and third rnds).
A Word to the Wise. Stop to make sure that your border lies flat.

3. With copper heather, sc into each sc along the top edge. Ch 1, turn and rep for 20 rows (5 inches).

4. Rep step 3 at the bottom and side edges.

5. With heather blue, sc a Fill-In Square into each corner space (beg the fill-in, with 20 sc down along one edge, and 20 sc up along the adjoining edge).
A Word to the Wise. Look at your Fill-In Square from the side to make sure it lines up with the edge of the border. If it pulls in, begin again, with an extra stitch or two on the first row. If it seems fuller than the border, take off a few sts).

6. With denim blue tweed (beg anywhere), work a final rnd of sc. End rnd with sl st in first sc. Fasten off.

#9 Patience Double Nine-Patch

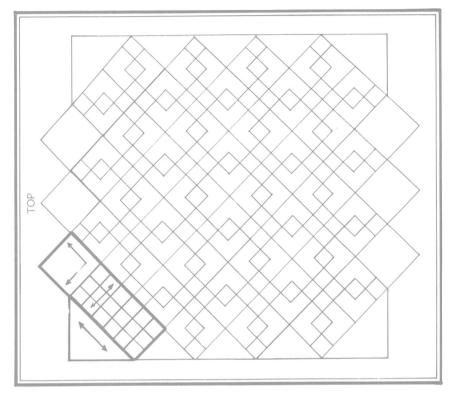

Here's another way to arrange color blocks within a Nine-Patch Checkerboard Grid. Quilters call this a Patience Nine-Patch pattern. We've built our afghan version around a double design unit, with the colors reversed from one half to the next. It's crocheted and pieced in strips and finished with a distinctive three-dimensional border. Patches Used: Checkerboard Grids, Fill-In Triangles, Fill-In Squares, Corner Triangles.

Directions
To Make the Double Nine-Patch Pattern Block
Ch 22 (7 lilac, 15 wine red).
Row 1: (Beg in 2nd ch from hook) 14 sc in wine red, 7 sc in lilac. Ch 1, turn now and throughout (21 sts).
Row 2: (Beg in first sc), 7 sc in lilac, 14 sc in wine red.
Rows 3–8: Cont to sc across, maintaining rows 1 and 2 color pattern.
Row 9: 7 sc in wine red, 7 sc in lilac, 7 sc in wine red.
Rows 10–16: Rep row 9.
Row 17: 7 sc in lilac, 14 sc in wine red.
Row 18: 14 sc in wine red, 7 sc in lilac.
Rows 19–24: Cont to sc across, maintaining rows 17 and 18 color pattern. (This completes first half of the pattern block).
A Word to the Wise. Stop to measure this first third of the unit to ensure all color blocks are equal.

Materials/Measurements
Finished Size: Approx. 40 by 52 inches.
Yarn: Coats & Clark Royal Mouline (wool worsted, 1.76-oz.) 8 lilac, 7 wine red, 4 dusty violet
Hook: Size I.
Gauge: 7 sts = 2 inches, 8 rows = 2 inches.
Each Double Nine-Patch unit = 6 by 12 inches.

Notes
• For a larger afghan, make additional strips, each with 2 more Patience Double Nine-Patch Units. Join your strips so that the 2 longest are always in the middle.
• Substitute any three shades from another color family or change the color effect completely by using three strongly contrasted colors—for example, light and dark blue plus beige, gold or white.

Row 25: 7 sc in wine red, 14 sc in lilac.

Row 26: 14 sc in lilac, 7 sc in wine red.

Rows 27–32: Cont to sc across, maintaining rows 25 and 26 color pattern.

Row 33: 7 sc in lilac, 7 sc in wine red, 7 sc in lilac.

Rows 34–40: Rep row 33.

Row 41: 14 sc in lilac, 7 sc in wine red.

Row 42: 14 sc in wine red, 7 sc in lilac.

Rows 43–48: Cont to sc across, maintaining rows 41 and 42 color pattern.

To Work and Join Double Nine-Patch Strips

1. Make 8 Double Nine-Patch Strips—2 strips each with 4, 3, 2 and 1 Double Nine-Patches.

2. Join 4 strips—a 4, 3, 2 and 1 Double Nine-Patch.

3. Rep step 2.

4. Join the 2 sets of pieced strips so that the colors are reversed as in the assembly diagram.

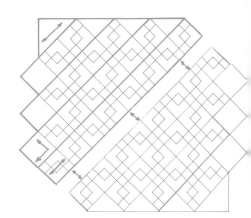

To Fill In Spaces at Top and Sides

1. With dusty violet, ridge st a Corner Triangle to the side edges of the 4 corner units (beg with 21 sts into each edge of the Double Nine-Patch).

2. With dusty violet, ridge st 6 Fill-In Triangles into the spaces at the top and bottom of the afghan (3 at each side—beg with 22 sts down along one edge and 22 sc sts from the corner up along the edge of the adjoining square).

3. With dusty violet, ridge st a Fill-In Square into the spaces at each side (3 each side—beg with same number of sts as Fill-In Triangle).

To Make Top and Bottom Border Strips

Row 1: With lilac (beg at top right edge with right side toward you), sc into the edge sts (reduce gauge to 13 sc for every 4 inches), until you get to the first Fill-In Square. *Beg at the Fill-In Square edge, ch 27, sk 27 sts (stretch ch in back of Fill-In Square), 1 sc. Rep from * 2 × and cont until you get to the corner. Ch 1, turn.

Row 2: Sc into each sc, including the unattached chs in back of the Fill-In-Triangles. Ch 1, turn.

Row 3: Sc into each sc across. Ch 1, turn.

Rows 4–25: Rep row 3 (border should extend an inch beyond the point of the Fill-In Square). Fasten off, then sew join the unattached foundation chs and the tips of the Fill-In Triangle Squares. Rep at the opposite side.

To Make Side Border Sections

Row 1: Turn the afghan sideways (with right side toward you, beg and end at the last row of the top and bottom border strips), sc into the edge sts in 13 st per four-inch gauge. Ch 1, turn.

Row 2: Sc into each sc across. Ch 1, turn.

Rows 3–10: Rep row 2. Fasten off.

To Finish

With wine red (beg anywhere, right side toward you), sc from left to right (Corded Edge) into edge sts all around (3 sc into each corner). End rnd with sl st join.

Row-by-Row Patch Six/Sawtooth and Across Triangle Square

The Sawtooth is a triangle. To turn it into a square, you crochet a Corner Triangle across the diagonal edge. What's so handy about this patch is that you can put stripes in either the Sawtooth or the Across Triangle. You can even put stripes in both halves of the patch as we did for the border in project #28. Whatever your design arrangement, it works up smoothly as an individual unit or in strips.
Applications: Project #10 (as the main patch), #21 (Sawtooth half only), #28 (border).

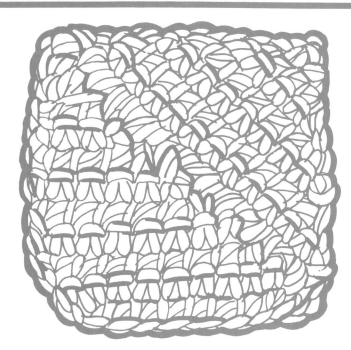

To Make Sample Patch
Ch 11.
Row 1: Sc into 2nd ch from hook and in each of 9 ch across. Ch 1, turn.
Row 2: Sc in each sc until 2 remain, dec (see *GENERAL IN-STRUCTIONS—Increasing and Decreasing*). Ch 1, turn.
Row 3: Work 1 sc, dec, sc across. Ch 1, turn.
Rows 4—10: Rep rows 2 and 3. Complete last yo in color to beg the Across Triangle. Ch 1 and turn patch sideways.

To Work the Across Triangle
Row 1: Work a sc into 15 sc evenly spaced along the diagonal edge. Ch 1, turn.
Row 2: Sc into each sc, working a dec at the beg and end of row. Ch 1, turn.
Rows 3—8: Rep row 2.

To Work the Patch as a Continuous Strip
Complete the last yo of the Across Triangle in color to beg next Sawtooth Triangle Square.
Row 1: Work 10 sc into the edge (beg at the end of the Across Triangle).
Rows 2—10: Rep rows 2—10 as in first Sawtooth section.

#10 Roman Stripe Sawtooth Quilt

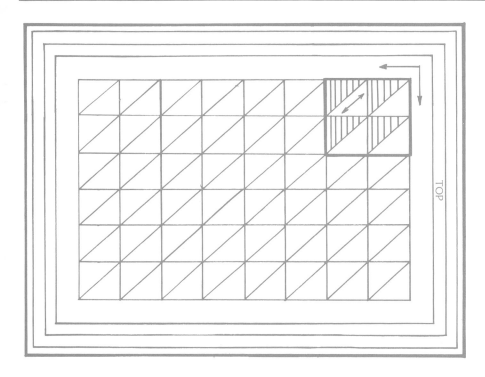

Traditionally Roman Stripe quilt patterns, also known as Shadow Squares, feature a dark solid and a diagonally striped triangle. By using bright colors and the Sawtooth and Across Triangle Square as our quilt motif, we've created a Roman Stripe pattern which reverses the traditional solid and striped arrangement. The result, while not as unmistakably nautical as the Tapestry Stitch Sailboat pattern in the Sampler (#35), nevertheless gives a distinct feeling of sails flapping in the breeze. A perfect project for a boy's room. Patches Used: Sawtooth Triangle and Across Square.

Materials/Measurements
Finished Size: Approx. 48 by 66 inches.
Yarn: Coats & Clark Royal Mouline (wool knitting worsted, 1.76-oz) 19 white, 8 each wine red, beige, royal blue, light blue.
Hook: Size I.
Gauge: 7 sts = 2 inches
4 rows = 1 inch
Each = 6 inches square,
8 inches on the diagonal.

Notes
• If you prefer the more traditional Roman Stripe look, work the Sawtooth Triangle in one color (a deep brown, burgundy or navy would be appropriate), then ridge stitch the Across Triangle in deep stripes.
• For an afghan that straddles past AND present, use a heathery green for your solid section with blue, lavender and natural for your stripes.

Directions
The Sawtooth and Across Units
Make 6 Sawtooth and
Across strips with 8 pattern units per strip. Ridge st the Sawtooth for 24 rows (ch 24 to beg). Sc the Across Triangle for 16 rows (beg with 31 sc spaced evenly across the diagonal edge). Switch colors at the end of every 4th row (2 ridges) of the Sawtooth Triangle, using the following color chart as a guideline for rotating the stripes from unit to unit.

Patch One
Color 1 = royal blue
Color 2 = light blue
Color 3 = beige
Color 4 = wine red
Color 5 = beige
Color 6 = royal blue

Patch Two
Color 1 = light blue
Color 2 = beige
Color 3 = wine red
Color 4 = royal blue
Color 5 = wine red
Color 6 = light blue

Patch Three
Color 1 = beige
Color 2 = wine red
Color 3 = royal blue
Color 4 = light blue
Color 5 = royal blue
Color 6 = beige

Patch Four
Color 1 = wine red
Color 2 = beige
Color 3 = light blue
Color 4 = royal blue
Color 5 = light blue
Color 6 = wine red

Patch Five
Color 1 = royal blue
Color 2 = light blue
Color 3 = beige
Color 4 = wine red
Color 5 = beige
Color 6 = royal blue

Patch Six
Color 1 = light blue
Color 2 = beige
Color 3 = wine red
Color 4 = royal blue
Color 5 = wine red
Color 6 = light blue

Patch Seven
Color 1 = beige
Color 2 = wine red
Color 3 = royal blue
Color 4 = light blue
Color 5 = royal blue
Color 6 = beige

Patch Eight
Color 1 = wine red
Color 2 = beige
Color 3 = light blue
Color 4 = royal blue
Color 5 = light blue
Color 6 = wine red

To Join Strips and Make Border
Join the 6 strips and border as follows:

Round 1: With white (beg at any corner with right side toward you), sc into the edge all around (dec gauge to 13 sc for every 4 inches). End rnd with sl st join to first sc. Ch 1, turn.

Round 2: Sc in each sc around (3 sc into each corner sc), sl st in first sc. Ch 1, turn.

Round 3: Sc in each sc around. Ch 1, turn.

Rounds 4–10: Rep rnds 2 and 3 (switch to wine red).

Rounds 11–24: Ridge st in each st around (3 sts into each corner st on even-numbered rnds (switch to royal blue at the end of rnd 16, switch to light blue at the end of rnd 20). Fasten off.

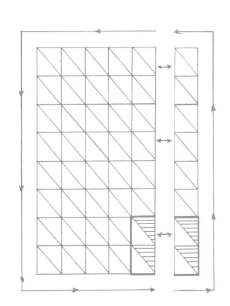

Row-by-Row Patch Seven/Double Triangle Square

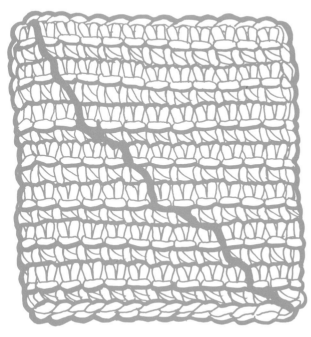

The Double Triangle is a crisp, fun-to-make patch. It resembles the Sawtooth and Across Triangle Square. However, it's crocheted all in one piece. If you stick to two colors, as we do throughout the book, you'll have no difficulty crocheting several Double Triangles in a single horizontal row.
Applications: Projects 11, 35 (squares 6 and 8).

To Make Sample Patch
With Color A, ch 11 plus a turning ch in B.
Row 1: With Color B, sc into the 2nd ch from the hook (the first color A); with Color A, sc in each of next 10 chs across. Ch 1, turn now and throughout.
Row 2: Sc in each sc—9 sc Color A, 2 Color B.
Row 3: 3 sc Color B, 8 sc Color A.
Row 4: 7 sc Color A, 4 sc Color B.
Row 5: 5 sc Color B, 6 sc Color A.
Row 6: 5 sc Color A, 6 sc Color B.
Row 7: 7 sc Color B, 4 sc Color A.
Row 8: 3 sc Color A, 8 sc Color B.
Row 9: 9 sc Color B, 2 sc Color A.
Row 10: 1 sc Color A, 10 Color B. Fasten off, or rep rows 1–10 to make a strip of Double Triangle Squares.

#11 Tree Everlasting

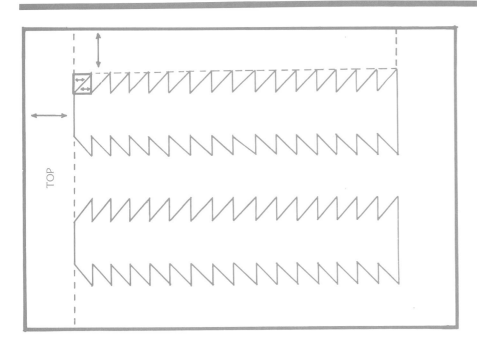

TOP

The names of many quilt patterns reflect the early American quilters' intense involvement with their religion. Tree Everlasting is a case in point. Other descriptive name tags often used include Arrowhead, Path of Thorns, Prickly Path and Herringbone. The "Tree's" graphic simplicity blends perfectly with traditional and modern furnishings. Our color scheme and the sturdy yarn used would make it a great wall hanging. If you sew it up with a sewing machine, as we did, you'll get it done in time to brighten your home for Christmas even if you're reading this with holiday music already ringing through the air.
Patches Used: Plain Patch strips, Double Triangles.

Materials/Measurements
Finished Size: Approx. 35 by 50 inches.
Yarn: Talon American "Dawn Sayelle" (4 ply orlon, 3½-oz.) 7 white, 8 red.
Hook: Size I.
Gauge: 4 sts = 1 inch, 11 rows = 2½ inches. Each Double Triangle = 2½ inches square. Each Plain Patch = 5" wide.

Notes
• Lengthen the strips for a longer afghan. Add a Plain Patch and a Double Triangle strip for more width.
• The little dashes of one color that pop up along the edge of the opposite color triangle are typical of Tapestry Stitch crochet. If you prefer a "dash-less" finish, work a running stitch over the dashes or select more subtly contrasted yarn colors.
• While the red and white combination used here is a favorite, any well matched pair of colors will look good—red and yellow, blue or brown with green. It's hard to go wrong.
• If you enjoy making Double Triangle Strips, you might follow it up with an ALL Double Triangle afghan, bordered with the double shell used in project #33.

Directions
1. Sc 3 red and 2 white Plain Patches (5 inches by 40 inches, 20 sts per row).
2. Sc 2 red Plain Patches (5 inches by 35 inches).
3. Make 4 strips with 16 Double Triangles each (ch 11 in white and a turning ch in red).

4. Assemble the 40-inch strips in this order: Red Plain Patch, Double Triangle, white Plain Patch, Double Triangle, red Plain Patch, Double Triangle, white Plain Patch, Double Triangle, red Plain Patch (flip 2 of the Double Triangle strips over to form the "tree branches").

5. Join strips. If you have a sewing machine you can join with zig-zag sts.

6. Join one of the shorter red Plain Patch strips to the top edge of the joined pieces and another to the bottom edge.

A Word to the Wise. Keep measuring units against each other as you work. Make doubly sure that the top and bottom patches fit comfortably across the edges (add extra rows if there's any pulling and take off rows if these borders ripple).

7. (Optional) sc around from left to right for a Corded Edge (3 sc into each corner st). End rnd with sl st join. Fasten off.

8. (Optional) with red, make 2 forty-inch casings (see *GENERAL INSTRUCTIONS—Casings for Hanging Afghans*). Join the casings to the top and bottom at the back.

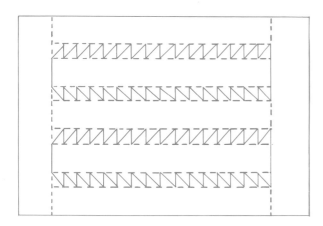

Row-by-Row
Patch Eight/Triple Triangle

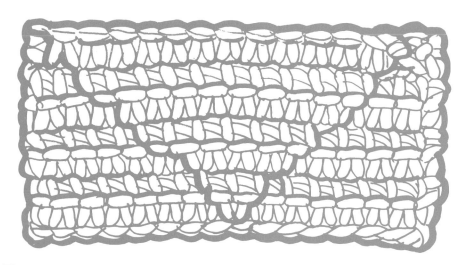

The Triple Triangle is a versatile patch. It can stand on its own
as the main motif for an afghan and also combines well with other
patches. In case you haven't noticed already, this winsome little patch
is really two Double Triangles with the colors positioned so that two
small triangles fall on either side of a larger central one.
Applications: Projects #12, 13, 14, 15, 35 (square 17).

To Make Sample Patch
Ch 18 (8 color A, 1 Color B, 9 Color A).
Row 1: (Right side toward you, on this and all odd-numbered rows)
with Color A, sc into 2nd ch from hook and each of next 7 chs;
with Color B, sc in next ch; with Color A, sc in each of next 8 chs.
Ch 1, turn now and throughout.
Row 2: (Wrong side toward you, on this and all even-numbered
rows), sc in each sc across—7 Color A, 3 Color B, 7 Color A.
Row 3: 6 sc Color A, 5 sc Color B, 6 sc Color A.
Row 4: 5 sc Color A, 7 sc Color B, 5 sc Color A.
Row 5: 4 sc Color A, 9 sc Color B, 4 sc Color A.
Row 6: 3 sc Color A, 11 sc Color B, 3 sc Color A.
Row 7: 2 sc Color A, 13 sc Color B, 2 sc Color A.
Row 8: 1 sc Color A, 15 Color B, 1 Color A. Fasten off, or rep
Rows 1–8 for a second Triple Triangle.

Remember

• When you switch colors, always complete last st in color to be dropped with yo in next color.

• Always carry along and crochet around yarn you'll be using again in the same row. Tug at the carried yarn end before you switch back to it (or look up the Stretch-In-the-Back method described in *GENERAL INSTRUCTIONS—Tapestry Stitch Color Changes*).

• If you use sharply contrasted yarns, you'll have some small dashes between the triangles. This is part of the Tapestry Stitch look. If you want to play this down, use soft, heathery colors.

To Crochet a Strip of Triple Triangles

1. Finish the yo for the last Row 8 st in Color B, ch 1 and turn.

2. Rep first row 2 × (The reason you do row 1 twice is to keep the triangle point nice and sharp).

3. Rep rows 2–8 of the Triple Triangle pattern unit.

Note: You can also start a Triple Triangle at the widest part of the larger triangle unit. This works best when the Triple Triangle is worked to an existing base (like some of the squares in project #35).

#12 Flying Geese

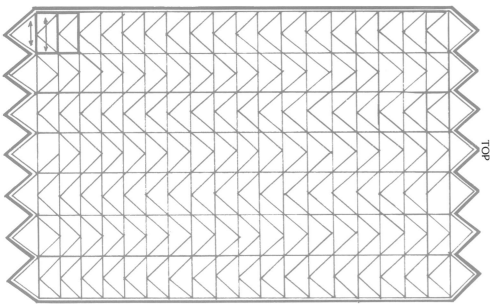

Flocks of birds migrating to a more favorable climate are the inspirational wellspring for one of the most appealing quilt patterns, Flying Geese. Every quilt show is sure to have at least three or four examples, possibly with other names such as Flocks of Birds, Ocean Waves, and Birds in the Air. In our cloud-soft baby afghan the pattern strips are arranged so that the "geese" head alternately south and north. The Corner Triangles crocheted to the top and bottom edge are called Prairie Points.

Patches Used: Triple Triangles, Corner Triangles.

Materials/Measurements
Finished Size: Approx. 35 by 51 inches.
Yarn: Phildar "Dedicace" (2 ply acrylic/mohair/wool 1¾-oz.) 10 each, Aurore (Color A), Ocean (Color B), 4 Liseron (Color C)— *each color used double stranded.*
Hook: Size I
Gauge: 17 sts = 4½ inches
9 rows = 2 ½ inches
Each pattern unit = 4½ by 2½ inches
Special Abbreviations: #1 pattern block = Triple Triangle with Color A center triangle.
#2 pattern block = Triple Triangle with Color B center triangle.

Notes
• Remember to start Triple Triangles at the point of the center triangle. It's easier.
• To lengthen the afghan, add more units to each strip. To widen it, add more strips. You can also enlarge the individual motifs by starting out with more stitches.
• With different colors, Flying Geese is as appropriate to an adult bedroom or living room as a nursery. For a rustic feeling, use brown and cream for the Triple Triangles and red to join and edge. To suggest birds flying over the ocean, use shades of silver with blue. For an extra bright afghan consider the colors used in 1910 Flying Geese pattern—navy and orange edged with gold and orange.

Directions

1. Sc 4 strips with 18 #1 pattern blocks and 3 strips with 18 #2 pattern blocks. Ch 18 to beg each strip, then work 17 sc each row. *A Word to the Wise.* Remember that the first Triple Triangle in each strip is made with 8 rows and all subsequent Triple Triangles with 9 rows (you repeat row 1 for a more clearly defined point).

2. With Color B, edge the side of each strip with a row of sc worked in a decreased gauge of 13 sc for every 4 inches.

3. Assemble the strips in alternating order (beg and end with a #1 pattern strip—position the #1 pattern strips with the center triangle pointing down and the #2 pattern strips with the center triangles pointing up).

4. Place 2 strips together with the right sides facing out and sl st join with Color C.

5. With Color C, sc a Corner Triangle to the top and bottom of each strip (beg with 17 sc).

6. With Color B (right side toward you), sc into edges all around (3 sc into the Corner Triangle points, sk 1 at the corners where the Corner Triangles adjoin). End rnd with sl st join to first sc. Ch 1. Cont around four more times (switch to Color A for third rnd, then back to Color B). Fasten off.

#13 Lightning Rods

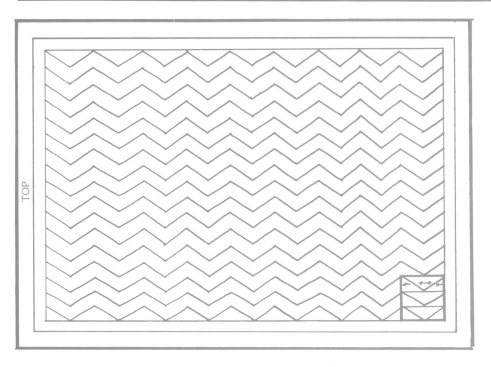

The zig-zag stripes that distinguish Lightning Rod or Streak O'Lightning patterns are crocheted in Triple Triangle strips. When everything is pieced together, the afghan is turned sideways to display the Lightning Rods to their most dramatic advantage. The slim all-around border is the only non-portable element.
Patches Used: Triple Triangles, Fill-In Triangles, Corner Triangles.

Materials/Measurements
Finished Size: Approx. 52 by 58 inches.
Yarn: Bernat Sesame "4" Heathers (wool knitting worsted, 3½-oz.) 3 balls each misty blue, oyster white, camel, light oxford grey, dark oxford grey, denim blue, claret, grape.
Hook: Size I.
Gauge: 7 sts = 2 inches
8 rows = 2 inches.
Each Triple Triangle = 6 by 3 inches.

Notes
• Remember, the Triple Triangle strips are turned sideways to display the Lightning Rod pattern. Consequently, you crochet additional pattern strips for a longer afghan and longer strips with more Triple Triangles for more width.
• All the strips in our sample are made in the same color sequence. You can also change colors from stripe to stripe for a broken zig-zag effect.
• Use as many colors as you want but repeat at least a couple to bind the pattern together.

Directions

1. Sc 9 "Lightning Rod" strips with 16 Triple Triangles (21 sc per row). Work each strip in the following color combinations:

Triple Triangle #1   = grape/misty blue/grape
Triple Triangle #2   = misty blue/oyster white/misty blue
Triple Triangle #3   = oyster white/camel/oyster white
Triple Triangle #4   = camel/misty blue/camel
Triple Triangle #5   = misty blue/dark oxford grey/ misty blue
Triple Triangle #6   = dark oxford grey/denim blue/dark oxford grey
Triple Triangle #7   = denim blue/light oxford grey/denim blue
Triple Triangle #8   = light oxford grey/claret/light oxford grey
Triple Triangle #9   = claret/camel/claret
Triple Triangle #10 = camel/oyster white/camel
Triple Triangle #11 = oyster white/misty blue/oyster white
Triple Triangle #12 = misty blue/denim blue/misty blue
Triple Triangle #13 = denim blue/dark oxford grey/denim blue
Triple Triangle #14 = dark oxford grey/light oxford grey/dark oxford grey
Triple Triangle #15 = light oxford grey/grape/light oxford grey
Triple Triangle #16 = grape/claret/grape

2. Sew join strips so that the "lightning rods" line up exactly (use yarn to match edge colors).
3. With claret and larger sized hook (right side toward you), sc into the edge sts all around (3 sc into each corner st). End rnd with sl st join to first sc. *Ch 1. Ridge st into each st around, sl st to first st, rep from *6 × (once each in claret, grape, oyster white, grape, twice more in claret). Fasten off.

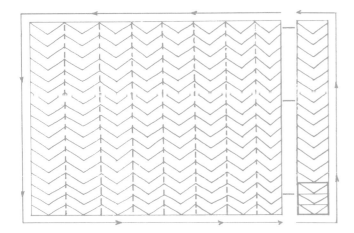

Granny
Patches
and

Projects

Granny squares and crochet go together like apples and pie crust. The Granny begins with a circle of stitches and grows in rounds. We've devised several working techniques especially suited to afghans with quilt motifs. Be sure to read the information that follows on how to begin Granny Patches and how to end Granny Patch rows. It applies to all projects.

Granny Patches and Projects

The Loosened Slip Knot To Begin Granny Patches

The traditional way to begin a Granny is to join the beginning and end of the foundation chain with a slip stitch. Then crochet as many stitches as you need for the first round into the ring.

Because afghans with quilt motifs look best with a tight, flat center, the following method is recommended: Make a slip knot but, instead of pulling it into a tight knot, leave an approximately ½-inch opening. Directions for this will read "make a loosened slip knot." With the double layered part of the slip knot between your thumb and forefinger, chain 1, single crochet into the loosened slip knot (insert the hook underneath the double layer of yarn), and repeat as many times as needed. Take hold of the beginning yarn end and pull to tighten the center, then chain one and slip stitch in the first sc (skip the chain one) to form a ring of stitches.

To End Granny Patch Rounds

All Granny Rounds end with a slip stitch join. Because our Grannies are all worked in single crochet and ridge stitches, that slip stitch is made into the first single crochet or ridge stitch made, *skipping the chain one.*

Our Granny Patches also feature an additional technique for moving from round to round. The technique with which you're probably most familiar, is referred to throughout these pages as the Up-and-Around method. After your slip stitch join at the end of the round, chain 1 and keep going around so that the right side of the work is always toward you.

With the Chain-and-Turn method you chain 1, turn and work back around with the wrong side of the patch toward you. This makes the end of the round easier to see and it produces stitches that will match those in Row-by-Row patches, an important consideration when both types of patches are used in a pattern.

While these methods are usually interchangeable, project directions specify the method that's either easier or more appropriate for each project. Round-by-round instructions are in the sections describing each patch. Instructions specific to a particular afghan are incorporated into the project directions.

To estimate the overall size when Center-Out Squares are set on the diagonal, use the point-to-point measurement of each patch as your yardstick. To figure out the number of squares needed for a specific size, see the Diagonal Set diagram in *GENERAL INSTRUCTIONS—Pattern "Sets" and Size Adjustments.*

Granny Patch One/Solid Center-Out Square

This patch is the granny square equivalent of the Row-by-Row Plain Patch. It serves as a launching pad for scores of great designs and combines beautifully with other patches. It looks good set in straight rows or on the diagonal to form a diamond square. Applications: Projects #14-16, 19-21, 35 (squares 13–15).

To Make Sample Patch (Up-and-Around Method)

Make a loosened slip knot as detailed in the introduction to this section, ch 1, 3 sc into the slip knot (insert hook underneath double layer of slip knot), ch 1 sl st in first sc to form ring (4 sts). Ch 1.

Round 1: 3 sc into each sc. End rnd with sl st in first sc. Ch 1 (12 sts, 4 corners made).

Round 2: 2 sc into first sc, *1 sc in each of next 2 sc, 3 sc in next sc, sc in each of next 2 sc. Rep from * 2 ×. End rnd with sl st in first sc. Ch 1. (20 sts).

Round 3: 2 sc into last sc, *1 sc in each of next 4 sc, 3 sc in next sc. Rep from * 2 ×. End rnd with sl st in first sc. Ch 1. (28 sts).

Round 4: 2 sc into 1st sc, 1 sc in each of next 6 sc *3 sc in next sc, 1sc in each of next 6 sc. Rep from * 2 ×. End rnd with sl st in first sc. (36 sts). Fasten off, or cont in above pattern of 8 inc per rnd (2 additional sc at each corner).

To Make Sample Patch (Chain-and-Turn Method)

Make loosened slip knot, ch 1, 3 sc into sl knot, sl st in first sc to form ring. Ch 1.

Round 1: 3 sc in each sc. End rnd with sl st in first sc. Ch 1, turn. (12 sts).

Round 2: (Wrong side toward you on this and all even-numbered rnds) 1 sc in each of first 2 sc, *3 sc in next sc, 1 sc in each of next 2 sc. Rep from * 2 ×, 2 sc in next sc. End rnd with sl st in first sc (sk sl st join and ch-1). Ch 1, turn (20 sts).

Round 3: 1 sc in first sc *3 sc in next st, 1 sc in each of next 4 sc. Rep from * 2 ×, 1 sc in each of next 3 sc, sl st in first sc. Ch 1, turn (28 sts).

Round 4: 1 sc into each of first 4 sc, *3 sc in next sc, 1 sc in each of next 6 sc. Rep from * 2 ×, 1 sc in last sc, sl st in first sc. Ch 1, turn (36 sts).

Round 5: 1 sc in each of first 2 sc, *3 sc into next sc, 1 sc in each of next 8 sc. Rep from *2 ×, 1 sc in each of next 5 sc. End rnd with sl st join (44 sts). Fasten off, *or* Ch 1, turn and cont in above pattern (1 sc in each sc to first corner *3 sc in next sc, 1 sc in each sc to next corner. Rep from * 2 ×, 1 sc in each sc to end of rnd, sl st join. Ch 1, turn.) *If you continue beyond round five, make corner increases on alternate rounds only.*

#14 Giant Stars

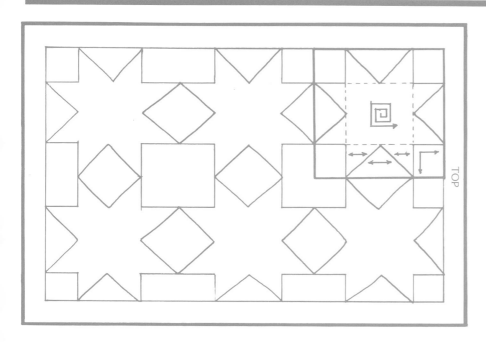

If you're a reasonably fast crocheter and give it about two hours a day, you should be able to polish off this celestial pattern in 7 days—one day for each Giant Star design block, and one to join the patches and make the border. Note how a second geometric pattern forms as the stars are joined.
Patches Used: Solid Center-Out Squares, Triple Triangles, Fill-In Squares.

Materials and Measurements
Finished Size: approx. 36 by 54 inches.
Yarn: Scheepjeswol Superwash Zermatt (wool worsted, 1¾-oz.) 18 white (#4812), 15 blue (#4838), 6 red (#4845)—*Use triple stranded.*
Hook: Size K.
Gauge: 2 sts = 1 inch, 3 rows = 1 inch.
Each star = 17 inches.

Notes
• If you prefer a lighter crochet fabric, use the yarn single stranded. This will produce a smaller square so that you will need 3 squares for each row. If you alternate the blue and white Stars with white Plain Patches, you can still finish the afghan in a jiffy.
• Remember, the border gauge is based on a rule of thumb. Check it out to see if any adjustments are needed.
• Consider the combination used for the Broken Star (#6) as a color alternative. For a softer palette, check out Patience Double Nine Patch (#8).

Directions

The Giant Star
Make 6

1. With white, ridge st a Center-Out Granny Square (10-inches square). Use the Chain-and-Turn method (2 ridge sts into sts before and after each corner st on alternate rnds).
2. Ridge st a Triple Triangle to each edge (beg with 11 white, 1 blue, 11 white sts).
3. With blue, sc a Fill-In Square in between the Triple Triangles (beg the patch with 10 sc sts into side edge of two adjoining Triple Triangles).

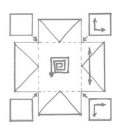

To Join Patches and Make Border

1. Join 2 completed star units across and 3 down.
A Word to the Wise. When working with heavy yarn a secure join is especially important.
2. With red (start at any corner, with right side toward you), sc all around (switch to a gauge of 11 sc for every 5 inches). End rnd with a sl st join in first sc. Ch 1, turn.
3. Sc back around (2 sc into each sc before and after corner sc). Ch 1, turn.
4. Lay afghan flat and adjust above gauge if necessary, then rep steps 2 and 3 for three inches. Fasten off.

#15 Cross

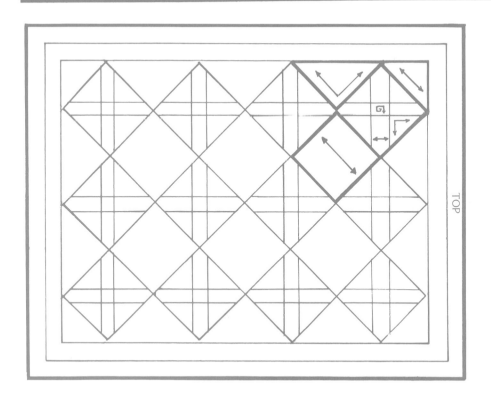

The electrifying colors of this afghan are true to the 18th century quilt which inspired it. The original was big and square with corner cutouts so it would fit a four poster bed. Ours is a rectangular throw made with two alternating blocks, a multi-patch Cross plus a solid-color Plain Patch. While some fabric quilters have pieced this pattern in straight rows, the "diagonal set" is more sophisticated. And, thanks to our trusty fill-in patches, the Corner and Fill-in Triangle, it's a breeze to execute.

Patches Used: Center-Out Squares, Plain Patches, Corner Triangles, Fill-In Triangles.

Materials/Measurements
Finished Size: Approx. 48 by 65 inches.
Yarn: Talon American (4 ply Dawn Sayelle knitting worsted 3½-oz.) 8 royal blue, 3 white, 2 each copper and dark gold.
Hook: Size I.
Gauge: 11 sts = 3 inches, 5 rows = 1 inch.
Each pattern block = 10 inches square.

Notes
• Take time to measure your patches against each other to ensure that they'll line up when joined.
• When you get to the fill-ins, bear in mind that you can work them without breaking off the yarn (sl st from finishing point of one unit to beg of next).
• To enlarge pattern, follow the assembly diagram for project #8 or the diagonal set diagram in *GENERAL INSTRUCTIONS.*
• If your taste runs to more understated colors, try a rust, brown and gold Cross and eggshell Plain Patch. Another pleasing possibility would be bright red with soft yellow and medium blue for the Cross square and a pale turquoise for the Plain Patch.

Directions
The Cross Pattern Squares
Make 12
1. With white, sc a Center-Out Square (3¼ inches square, 44 sts all around. Use the Up-and-Around method (do not turn at the end of the rnd).
2. With copper, *11 ridge sts into edge sts along one side of the white square. Ch 1, turn. Rep from * for 20 rows with 10 ridges on each side (4 inches).
3. Complete the cross bar with a Corner Triangle (ridge st for 5 rows with a dec at the beg and end of each row).

4. Rep steps 2 and 3 at the other three edges of the white square.

5. With gold, sc 4 Fill-In Triangles between the cross bars. Beg the fill-in just below the triangle points (14 sc evenly spaced down along one edge, 14 sc up along the adjoining bar's edge).

6. With royal blue, sc 4 Corner Triangles to the top and bottom edges (beg each triangle with 35 sc into edge sts).

7. With royal blue, sc Fill-In Triangles into the spaces between the Cross and Plain Patch units (3 fill-ins at each long side and 2 each at each short side—each starting with 35 sc into the edge sts of two adjoining Crosses).

8. (Optional) Surface Crochet (see GENERAL INSTRUCTIONS) all around the inside edges of the Corner and Fill-In Triangles with blue yarn. Make 3 sc sts in the sts at the triangle points. When you get to where the points of the Fill-In Triangle and the Plain Patch meet, attach with a sl st through the middle ch.

The Plain Patches

Make 6

With royal blue, ch 37.

Row 1: 36 sc. Ch 1, turn now and throughout.

Rep row 1 until square measures 10 inches.

A Word to the Wise. Stop after the first few rows to make sure that the edges of the Plain Patch and the Cross pattern block line up.

To Join and Fill in The Edges

1. Follow the assembly diagram to arrange and join the patches into 4 rows of alternating Cross and Plain Patch blocks (2 rows with 5 blocks and 2 with 3 blocks),

2. Join a Cross block to the middle block of each end row.

To Make the Border

Round 1: (Right side toward you) with white, sc into edge sts all around (in decreased gauge of 13 sc per 4 inches). End rnd with sl st join. Lay afghan flat to check gauge and adjust if necessary. Ch 1, turn.

Round 2: (Wrong side toward you) sc in each sc around (3 sc into each corner st), sl st in first sc. Ch 1, turn.

Rounds 3—4: Rep rnds 1 and 2 (yo last st on rnd 4 in copper to switch color).

Rounds 5—6: Rep rnds 1 and 2 (switch to gold).

Rounds 7—8: Rep rnds 1 and 2 (switch to blue).

Rounds 9—10: Rep rnds 1 and 2 (switch to white).

Rounds 11—14: Rep rnds 1—4.

Round 15: (Optional) sc one rnd from left to right for Corded Edge (see *GENERAL INSTRUCTIONS*). Fasten off.

#16 Hole In The Barn Door

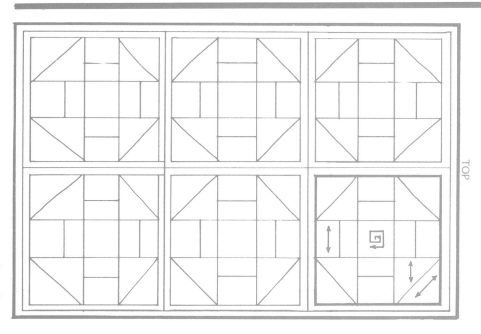

The history of American quilting abounds with names and images that reflect every day rural life. Hole in the Barn Door, also known as Churning, is one of the most beloved and crochetable. Like the previous project, this one begins with a Center-Out Square. In this instance, the square is built into a long strip. Several patches are then worked all as one along each side.

Patches Used: Center-Out Squares, Plain Patches, Sawtooth and Across Triangles.

Materials/Measurements
Finished Size: Approx. 39 by 58 inches.
Yarn: Coats & Clark Red Heart "Preference" (4 ply orlon, 3½-oz.) 5 boardwalk blue, 3 each bisque and taupe, 2 each white and olympic blue.
Hook: Size I.
Gauge: 3 sts = 1 inch, 4 rows = 1 inch.
Each "barn door" square = 15 inches square,
17 inches square when bordered.

Notes
• For a larger afghan, make 9 Barn Door squares and add one to each row. To make this larger size without spending a lot of extra time, make just 5 Barn Door squares and alternate them with 4 boardwalk blue Plain Patches.
• For a change of color, whitewash the barn with off-white and make the sky a deep purple OR, abandon realism altogether for fantasy pinks, blues or greens.

Directions
To Make the Central Pattern Strip
Make 6
1. With boardwalk blue and the Chain-and-Turn method, sc a Center-Out Granny Square (44 sts, 3 inches square).
2. With taupe, work 11 ridge sts into one edge of the Center-Out Square. Ch 1, turn. *11 ridge sts. Ch 1, turn. Rep from * 3 × in taupe, 4 × in bisque, 4 × in taupe (2 ridges each color—switch to boardwalk blue on last taupe yo).
3. With boardwalk blue, work 12 rows (ridge st the first row, sc the rest). Fasten off.
4. Rep steps 1–3 at the opposite side of the Center-Out Square.

The Sawtooth Triangle/Plain Patch Section

Make 1 for each side of the central strip

Turn the strip sideways.

Row 1: With bisque, work 11 sc into the edge sts of the boardwalk blue color block, 12 sc into the striped block edge sts; with taupe, 1 ridge st in each of the next 12 sts (the Center-Out Square edge): with bisque, 12 sc in striped block edge sts, 11 sc in last boardwalk blue edge sts. Ch 1, turn now and throughout. (This is the foundation for the pattern square of a Plain Patch and 2 Sawtooth Triangles and Across.)

Rows 2–4: With colors in same pattern as previous row, work 1 ridge st into each st across. (Dec 1 st at beg of each Sawtooth Triangle edge now and throughout, see *GENERAL INSTRUCTIONS—Increasing and Decreasing*.)

Rows 5–8: Rep rows 2–4 procedure but use taupe where you used bisque and bisque where you used taupe.

Rows 9–12: In row 1–4 color pattern, 1 ridge st into each st across.

Row 13: With taupe, 1 ridge st in each bisque st; with boardwalk blue, 1 sc in each of next 12 sts; with taupe, 1 ridge st in each of next bisque sts

Rows 14–15: Rep row 13 color and st pattern.

Rows 16–20: Rep rows 13–15 but with beige where you used taupe. (This leaves 1 st at each Sawtooth edge).

The "Across" Triangle for the "Sawtooth"

Make 4 per Barn Door square

With boardwalk blue, work 29 sc evenly across the diagonal edge of the striped Sawtooth, then dec at the beg and end of each row until 1 st remains.

The Barn Door Borders

Round 1: With boardwalk blue (beg at any corner, with wrong side toward you), sc into the edge sts all around (dec gauge to 13 sc per 4 inches), sl st in first sc. Ch 1, turn.

Round 2: With white, 1 sc into each sc (3 sc into each corner sc), sl st in first sc. Ch 1, turn.

Rounds 3–4: Rep rnds 1 and 2 (switch to olympic blue for last rnd). Fasten off.

To Join and Finish

Assemble the Barn Door Squares in rows (2 squares across, 3 rows) then border all around.

Round 1: With olympic blue (beg at any corner, right side toward you), sc into edges all around (13 sc per 4-inch gauge). End rnd by switching to white and sl st in first sc. Ch 1, turn.

Round 2: Sc in each sc (3 sc into each corner sc), sl st in first sc. Ch 1, turn.

Rounds 3 and 4: Rep rnds 1 and 2 (switch to olympic blue for last rnd). Fasten off.

Granny Patch Two/Multi-Color Center-Out Square

This is a variation of Granny Patch One. Instead of crocheting each of the square's triangular segments in the same color, you use two, three or even four colors. Instead of crocheting 3 stitches into the corner stitch, you work an increase at the beginning and end of each color segment. While this patch could be worked without turning at the end of each round, instructions focus on the Chain-and-Turn method as it simplifies color changes.
Applications: Projects #17, 18.

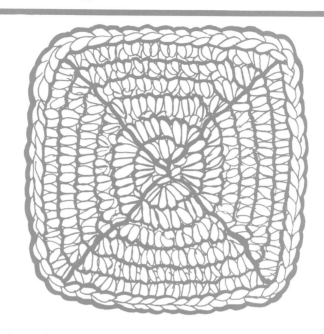

To Make Sample Patch

With Color A, make a loosened slip knot (see introduction to *GRANNY PATCHES AND PROJECTS*), ch 1, 3 sc into slip knot circle (1 Color A, 1 Color B, 1 Color A). Insert hook into first sc to form ring, slip stitching through in Color A (4 sts). Ch 1.

Round 1: 3 sc into each of first 3 sc (3 each Colors A, B, A). With B, 2 sc in next sc. End rnd with combination sc/sl st join made by inserting hook in same sc and again in first sc, then slip stitching through remaining lps on hook. Ch 1, turn (12 sts).

Round 2: (Wrong side toward you on this and all even numbered rnds) with Color B, *2 sc in first sc, 1 sc in next sc, 2 sc in next sc. Rep from * 2x (once each in Colors A and B). With Color A, 2 sc in first sc, 1 sc in each of next 2 sc. End rnd with combination sc/sl st join (insert hook into same sc yo and pull through ch lps so that 2 lps remain, insert hook into first sc of rnd, slip stitching through 2 lps). Ch 1, turn (5 sts each side of square—20 sts all around).

Round 3: With Color A, *2 sc into first sc, 1 sc in each of next 3 sc, 2 sc in next sc. Rep from * 2x (once each in Colors B and A). With Color B, 2 sc in first sc, 1 sc in each of next 3 sc, 1 sc in next sc. Sl st join last sc to first sc as in rnd 2. Ch 1, turn (7 sts each side of square—28 sts all around).

Round 4: With Color B, *2 sc into first sc, 1 sc in each of next 5sc, 2 sc in next sc. Rep from * 2x (once each in Colors A and B). With Color A, 2 sc in first sc, 1 sc in each of next 5 sc, 1 sc in next sc. Sl st join last sc to first sc as in rnd 2. Ch 1, turn (9 sts each side of square—36 sts all around).

Round 5: With Color A, *2 sc into first sc, 1 sc in each of next 7 sc, 2 sc in next sc. Rep from * 2x (once each in Colors B and A). With B, 2 sc in first sc, 1 sc in each of next 7 sc, 1 sc in next sc. Sl st join last sc to first sc as in rnd 2. Ch 1, turn (11 sts each side of square—44 sts all around).

Round 6: In colors to match previous rnd, sc all around. To avoid rippling, *do not inc on this and all even-numbered rnds.* Ch 1, turn.

Round 7: With Color B, *2 sc into first sc, 1 sc in each of next 9 sc, 2 sc in next sc. Rep from * 2x (once each in Colors A and B). With A, 2 sc in first sc, 1 sc in each of next 9 sc, 1 sc in next sc. Sl st join last sc to first sc as in rnd 2. Ch 1, turn (13 sts each side of square—52 sts all around).

For a larger patch cont in above pattern, with 1 inc at the beg and end of every segment on alternate rnds, ending rnds with combination sc/sl st join.

Remember

• Always bring up new color to use as the last yo of the old color.
• For Multi-Color Center-Out Squares with 2 colors (as per above), or 3 colors (as in project #17), always carry along yarn you'll be using again in the same round.
• For Multi-Color Center-Out Squares with 4 different colors, drop the yarn at the end of each segment (no need to carry and crochet around it).

#17 Bow Ties

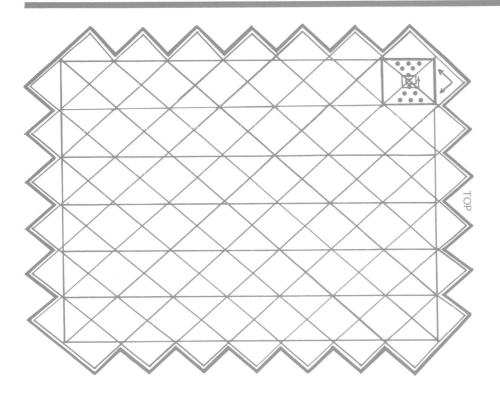

If you poke around fabric quilt pattern books, you'll discover quite a few patterns inspired by the bow tie, for many years the only item in a man's wardrobe for a touch of whimsy and self-expression. Our crocheted Bow Ties are polka dotted with picot stitches. Except for a few color switches in the bow tie segments, you just repeat the same unit until you have enough to piece it all together. The border is an encore of the Prairie Points introduced in the Flying Geese project (#12), except that here it encircles the entire afghan.
Patches Used: Multi-Color Center-Out Squares, Corner Triangles.

Materials/Measurements
Finished Size: Approx. 42 by 48 inches.
Yarn: Coats & Clark Royal Mouline (4 ply wool worsted 1.76-oz.) 3 each navy and white; 2 each red, dark grey and light grey.
Hook: Size I.
Gauge: 7 sts = 2 inches, 7 rounds = 2 inches.
Each square = 6 inches.
Special Abbreviation: BT = Color used for picot segments.

Notes
• To crochet the Prairie Point triangles without breaking off yarn, sl st from the point to the beg of the next Corner Triangle.

• Only the BT color needs to be carried around (when you work with white). Leave other colors hanging at the back and pick up when needed.
• Always bring up new color to use as the last yo the old color.
• Remember to end rounds with combination single crochet/slip stitch join—inserting hook into the last stitch of the last color segment and again through the first single crochet of the round, then slip stitching through the 2 loops on hook.
• You can make the squares without the picot stitches. While this plays down the bow tie effect, it also makes it more feasible to use just 2 colors or a different color for each segment (see notes headlined REMEMBER in the Sample Patch section).

Directions
Make 42 Multi-Color Center-Out Patches with "Polka Dot" Picots—12 with red BT color segments and dark grey picots, 12 with red BT color segments and light grey picots, 6 with light grey BT color segments and red picots, 6 with light grey BT segments and dark grey picots, 6 with dark grey BT segments and red picots. Beg each patch with a loosened slip knot in navy (ch 1, 3 sc into slip knot circle—1 each in BT, white, BT). Sl st join to first sc to form ring (sl st through in navy). Ch 1. Cont in rnds as follows:

Round 1: 12 sc all around (3 each in navy, BT, white, BT). End this and all rnds with sc/sl st join. Ch 1, turn now and throughout. (See *Granny Patch Two—To Make Sample Patch* for how to make sc/sl st join and step-by-step details through rnd 7.)

Round 2: (Wrong side toward you—inc at beg and end of each color) 20 sc (5 each BT, white, BT, navy).

Round 3: (Cont to inc at beg and end of each color) 28 sc all around (7 each navy, BT, white, BT).

Round 4: 36 sc all around (9 each BT, white, BT, navy).

Round 5: 44 sc all around (11 each navy, BT, white, BT). Tie 1–2 yard length of yarn for picots to first BT segment. Work 1 picot into 5th st of BT segment (complete 4th sc in picot color, ch 5, insert hook back into first ch, sl st through in BT color). Carry picot yarn with you and crochet around it until you get to second BT segment, then work another picot into the 5th st.

Round 6: (Do not increase) 44 sc all around (11 each BT, white, BT, navy). To lock in the picot made on the previous rnd so that it falls forward, press the picot against the front with your forefinger as you sc into the sts before and after the picot (fasten off the picot yarn).

Round 7: 52 sc (13 each BT, white, BT, navy). Rep rnd 5 procedure for working picot sts into BT segments on 4th and 6th sc of each segment.

Round 8: (Cont sample patch procedures now and through rnd 11) 52 sc all around in navy, BT, white, BT color sequence (do not inc). Rep rnd 6 procedure for locking in the picots made on rnd 5.

Round 9: With BT color, *2 sc into first sc, 1 sc in each of next 13 sc, 2 sc in next sc. Rep from * 2 × (once each in white and BT). With navy, 2 sc in next sc, 1 sc in each of next 13 sc, 1 sc in next sc. Rep rnd 5 procedure for working picots into 4th, 7th and 10th sc of the BT segments (15 sts each side, 3 picots on 2 sides, 60 sts all around).

Round 10: (Do not inc) 60 sc all around in navy, BT, white, BT color sequence. Rep rnd 6 procedure for locking in picots.

Round 11: With BT color, *2 sc into first sc, 1 sc in each of next 15 sc, 2 sc in next sc. Rep from * 2 × (once each in white and BT). With navy, 2 sc in next sc, 1 sc in each of next 15 sc, 1 sc in next sc. End rnd with combination sc/sl st join (17 sts each side, 68 sts all around).

Rounds 12 and 13: Rep rnd 11 color and inc sequence. Fasten off.

To Join Bow Tie Squares and Add Prairie Points

1. Join 6 matching squares to form a row.

2. Join rows so that every other one contains 2 red Triangles with picots.

3. With red, sc a Corner Triangle to the edge of each square (beg with 19 sts).

4. With navy, sc all around Corner Triangles (work 3 sc into the sts at the points, sk 1 st at each inside corner). Ch 1. Rep for a second rnd. Fasten off.

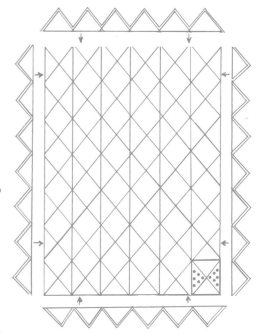

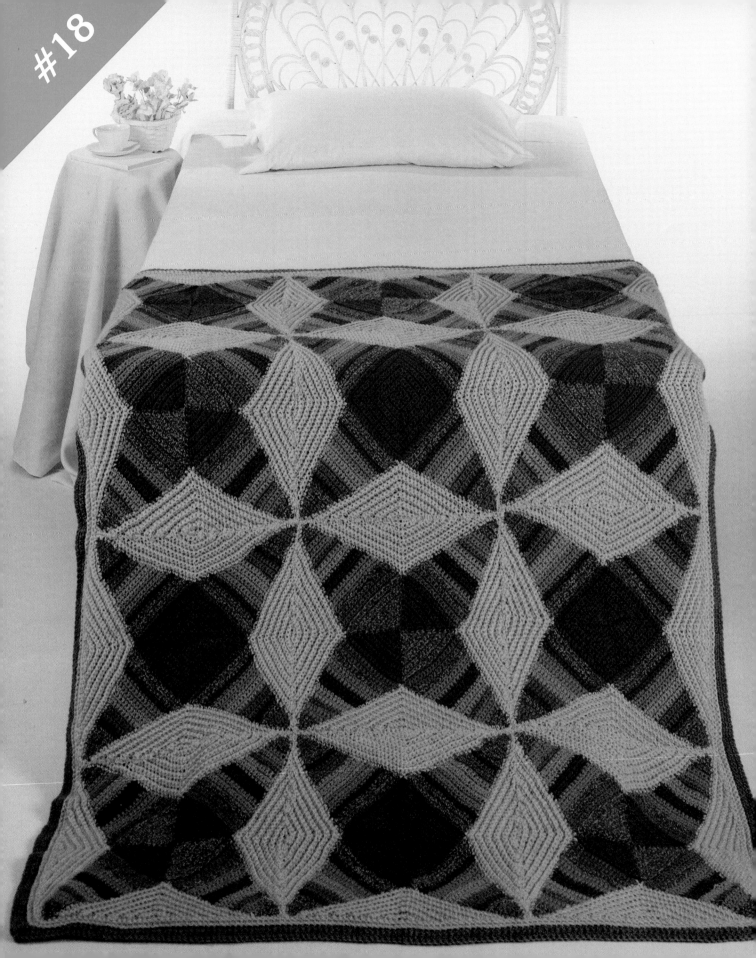

#18 Rocky Road to Kansas

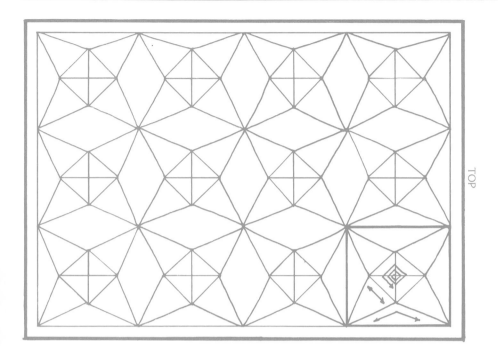

TOP

The way secondary patterns emerge when you piece some design units can be fascinating. Take the pink stars you see here. They look as if they were the primary design element but are in fact Fill-In Triangles—the last step for making the central design unit which begins with a Center-Out Square. Naturally, when one patch in a pattern block gets blown up during the piecing process, as the Fill-In Triangle does here, it's important to keep the overall pattern in mind when you choose your colors. The other triangular patch used in this pattern is a taller version of the Corner Triangle.

Patches Used: Solid and Multi-Color Center-Out Squares, Corner Triangles (tall), Fill-In Triangles.

Materials/Measurements
Finished Size: Approx. 49 by 69 inches.
Yarn: Phildar "Pegase 206" (4 ply acrylic and wool worsted, 1¾-oz.) 17 Eglantine (Color A), 7 Castor (Color B), 6 each Cosmos (Color C) and Nuage (Color D), 2 each Tamaris (Color E), Stratus (Color F).
Hook: Size I.
Gauge: 3 sts = 1 inch, 4 rows = 1 inch.
Each pattern square = 15 inches.

Notes
• To enlarge the afghan without making additional design blocks, widen the border two to four inches. Either continue all around or make a Strip and Square border as in projects #8 and 22.
• For greater color uniformity, make all the design blocks with Solid Center-Out Squares and the same color stripes. For more color diversity, add additional color combinations. Whatever you do about the colors for the Center-Out Squares and the Triangles, the Fill-In Triangles should always be in one color.
• For a more subdued look, substitute a soft lavender or pale blue for the pink. You can also reverse the color scheme by crocheting the basic design unit in pastels and the Fill-In Triangles in a dark shade.

Directions
The Rocky Road Pattern Square
Make 12: 6 starting with a solid Center-Out Square in Color C and 6 starting with a Multi-Color Center-Out Square in Color C and Color D.
1. Sc 6 solid-color Center-Out Squares in Color C with the Chain-and-Turn Method (6½ inches square, 84 sts all around).
A Word to the Wise. Remember to increase on alternate rounds only after the fifth round to prevent your patches from rippling.

2. Sc 6 Multi-Color Center-Out Squares in Color C and Color D (same size as solid-color square).

3. Sc a tall Corner Triangle to each edge of all squares (beg with 21 ridge sts into the square's edge, switch to sc to complete the triangle.) Follow the chart for color and dec sequence.

4. With Color A, ridge st a Fill-In Triangle between the striped triangles, from the point of one triangle to the point of the adjacent triangle. Because the triangles are so long, the fill-ins are wider than usual (beg with 28 sts into each edge).

5. Join 3 squares to form a row—2 rows alternating from solid-color to multi-color to solid color unit; 2 rows reversing this sequence. Join the 4 rows, again alternating from one color combination to the other.

6. With Color A, ridge st all around the joined squares in a reduced gauge of 11 sts for every 4 inches. End rnd with a sl st join. Ch 1, turn.

7. Ridge st back around (3 sc into each corner st), end rnd with sl st (yo in Color B). Ch 1, turn.

8. Rep steps 6 and 7 twice.

9. (Optional) with Color E, sc one rnd from left to right for Corded Edge. Fasten off.

Row-by-Row Color and Decrease Sequence for Tall Triangles (dec at the beg and end of each row containing an asterisk)

	Solid Center-Out Square	Multi-Color Center-Out Square
Row 1:	Color D	Color B
Row 2:	Color D	Color B
Row 3:	Color D *	Color B *
Row 4:	Color D	Color B
Row 5:	Color C	Color D
Row 6:	Color C *	Color D *
Row 7:	Color F	Color F
Row 8:	Color F	Color F
Row 9:	Color F *	Color F *
Row 10:	Color F	Color F
Row 11:	Color E	Color C
Row 12:	Color E *	Color C *
Row 13:	Color E	Color C
Row 14:	Color E	Color C
Row 15:	Color B *	Color E *
Row 16:	Color B	Color E
Row 17:	Color B	Color E
Row 18:	Color B *	Color E *
Row 19:	Color C	Color B
Row 20:	Color C	Color B
Row 21:	Color D *	Color F *
Row 22:	Color D	Color F
Row 23:	Color D	Color F
Row 24:	Color D *	Color F *
Row 25:	Color B	Color D
Row 26:	Color B	Color D
Row 27:	Color B *	Color D *
Row 28:	Color B	Color D
Row 29:	Color B	Color D
Row 30:	Color B *	Color D *

Granny Patch Three/Boxes

In project #4 you've already seen how you can transform a row of Plain Patches into a diamond pattern setting each square on its point. When Corner Triangles are added to individual Plain Patches set on the diagonal, they're called Boxes. Boxes are not for squares only. They can of course also be used to square off other shapes such as Octagons. Thus, they provide you with a convenient means for obtaining a straight joining edge, no matter what shape you begin with. While there's nothing to stop you from adding boxes to Plain Patches, you'll find they look best when the stitches flow from a Granny Patch that grows from the center out.
Applications: Projects #19, 20, 21 and 22.

To Make Sample Patch

1. Sc a Solid Center-Out Square (9 sts each edge, 36 sts all around.)
2. With contrast-colored yarn, work 11 ridge sts into one edge of square. Ch 1, turn.
3. Ridge st back along previous row with 1 dec at the beg and end (see *GENERAL INSTRUCTIONS—Increasing and Decreasing).*
Ch 1, turn and rep for 5 rows (until 1 st is left). Fasten off.
4. Rep steps 2 and 3 at other 3 sides.
Note: To crochet all 4 boxes without breaking off yarn, sl st from the end of one triangle to the beg of the next.

#19 Pieced T

TOP

Materials/Measurements
Finished Size: Approx. 48 × 48 inches.
Yarn: Phildar Pegase (4 ply acrylic and worsted, 1¾-oz.) 13 Tamaris (Color A), 12 Source (Color B).
Hook: Size I.
Gauge: 4 sts = 1 inch, 4 rows = 1 inch.
Each pattern square = 15 inches.

Notes
• For minimum show-through when switching colors, see the *GENERAL INSTRUCTIONS— Tapestry Stitch Color Changes.*
• For a larger, more rectangular afghan, add an extra row of pattern blocks. For a crib or carriage-sized afghan, make 6 instead of 9 units and join 2 per row for 3 rows (see projects #16 and 34).
• The T pattern will work well in practically any pair of colors, whether opposites or neighbors on the color wheel. For a more drastic color change, crochet each T in a different color but stick to one color for all the center-out squares.

The familiar letter T is vivid testimony to our grandmothers' ingenuity for arranging ordinary shapes into an endless variety of tasteful and timeless patterns. We've adapted what's probably the most popular of these T arrangements, the Double T, for interesting yet simple crocheting. It's all done with one pattern block made with a medley of patches to crochet join as you work. The reversal of colors from one block to the next creates an additional design element when everything is pieced. For a different approach to the fascinating T, see project #31. Patches Used: Solid Center-Out Squares, Boxes, Triple Triangles, Fill-In Triangles, Corner Triangles.

Directions
1. With Color A, sc a Center-Out Square (4 inches square). Use the Chain-and-Turn Method.
2. With Color B, sc a Box to each edge (beg each triangle with 15 sc into the edge sts).

3. Sc a double Triple Triangle to each boxed edge. (Beg with 9 sc Color B, 1 Color A, 9 Color B; end with 1 Color B, 17 Color A, 1 Color B). Each triangle is made with 9 rows (including the row worked into the Center-Out Square edge). The last row of the first triangle is made with the right side toward you; the last row of the 2nd triangle is made with the wrong side toward you.

4. With Color B, sc 4 Fill-In Triangles between the double Triple Triangles (beg with 13 sc into each edge, from the top edge of one double Triple Triangle down to the corner and up along the edge of the adjoining Triple Triangle).

5. With Color A, sc a Corner Triangle across each Fill-In Triangle (beg with 21 sc into the base of the Fill-In Triangle).

6. With Color A, sc all around with gauge decreased to 11 sts for every 4 inches (3 sc into each corner st).

7. Make 4 more squares in same colors and procedures as in steps 1–6.

8. Make 4 T Pattern squares using same procedures as steps 1 to 6, but reverse the colors (Center-Out Square in Color B, Boxes in Color A, Triple Triangles in A/B/A sequence, Fill-In Triangle in A and Corner Triangle and sc edging in B).

To Join and Border

1. Join pattern blocks into 3 rows with 3 alternating color blocks each (beg and end with a Color A Center-Out Square on rows 1 and 3 and with a Color B Center-Out Square on the middle row).

2. Join the rows.

3. With Colors A and B double stranded and larger hook, sc all around in gauge decreased to 11 sts for every 4 inches (3 sc into each corner sc). End rnd with sl st join to first sc. Ch 1 and cont for two more rounds. Fasten off.

A Word to the Wise. Lay work flat after each border round to make sure that the gauge is correct. If you see any rippling, go back and reduce the number of stitches at each side. If the border seems too tight, go back and increase the number of stitches.

#20 World Without End

World Without End links two different patterns. The one after which the afghan is named demonstrates how you can keep stacking Boxes, one on top of another. The second or linking pattern is a single crochet version of Project #14 Star pattern. The piecing process once again yields an intriguing secondary pattern, a Road running between the stars. You'll spot it, if you squint a bit, something quilters do all the time to see everything that's going on.

Patches Used: Solid Center-Out Squares, Boxes, Triple Triangles, Fill-In Squares, Corner Triangles.

Materials/Measurements
Finished Size: Approx. 50 by 65 inches.
Yarn: Phildar "Lenox 084" (wool worsted, 3½-oz.) 11 balls each Celestial (Color A), Titian (Color B), Baroque (Color C).
Hook: Size I.
Gauge: 7 sts = 2 inches, 8 rows = 2 inches.
Each pattern square = 15 inches square

Notes
Begin the afghan by making 1 of each pattern square. That way you can check to make sure each is the same size and that the interlocking corners will line up properly.
• When you make the Fill-In Squares for the star pattern, remember to turn your work sideways after the first two rows to ensure that the square's edges will line up with the top of the Triple Triangle. If the square seems skimpy, go back and add a few stitches to the foundation row. If it seems too full, use fewer stitches.
• Check out the *GENERAL INSTRUCTIONS—Pattern "Sets" and Size Adjustments* if you want to arrange the pattern blocks on the diagonal.
• For a brighter color format, substitute red for the Color A areas and emerald green for the areas now in Color B.

Directions
World Without End Pattern Squares
Make 6
1. With Color A, sc a Solid Center-Out Square with Chain and Turn Method (6 inches square).
A Word to the Wise. After round 5, work corner increases on alternate rounds only to prevent buckling.
2. With Color C, sc a Corner Triangle to each edge (beg with 19 ridge sts into the edge sts at one side; switch to sc to complete triangle).

3. With Color A, sc a Corner Triangle to each edge of the boxed Center-Out Squares (beg with 13 sc into the Color C edge sts, 1 sc into the Color A st in the middle, 13 sc into the last Color C edge sts).

4. With Color B, beg to sc a Corner Triangle to each edge, across the 2 adjoining Color A triangles (beg with 19 sc into the first Color A edge sts, 1 sc in the Color C st between the boxes, 19 sc in the second Color A edge sts). After 16 rows (17 sts), complete the triangle in Color A.

Star Pattern Square
Make 6
1. With Color A, sc a Solid Center-Out Square with Chain and Turn Method (8 inches square).
2. With Color C and B, work a Triple Triangle patch to each side, starting with a row of ridge sts and completing the patch in sc (beg with 14 Color C, 1 Color B, 14 Color C; end with 1 Color C, 27 Color B, 1 Color C).
3. With Color A, sc a Fill-In Square into each space between two Triple Triangles (beg with 11 sc into each edge).

To Join
1. Edge each square with one rnd of sc sts all-around, in yarn color to match edge sts.
2. Join patches into 4 rows of 3 alternating pattern squares.
3. Join rows (alternate a World/Star/World row with a Star/World/Star row).

To Make Border
Round 1: With Color C, sc all around in gauge decreased to 13 sts for every 4 inches. End rnd with sl st join in first sc. Ch 1, turn.
Round 2: Sc into each sc around (3 sc into each corner sc—finish last yo in Color B to switch color), sl st in first sc. Ch 1, turn.
Rounds 3–6: With Color B, rep rnd 1 (switch to Color C at end of last rnd).
Rounds 7 and 8: Rep rnds 1 and 2. Fasten off.

Granny Patch Four/ All-Around and Half-Way-Around Fences

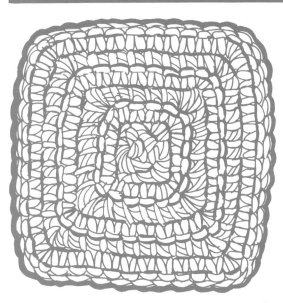
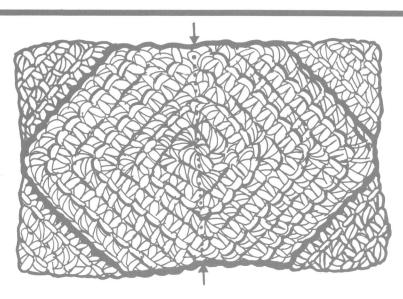

To add yet another dimension to the Center-Out Square, turn it on its point and surround it with contrast-colored stripes, then square off the corners with Boxes. In quilt language, such stripes are known as Fences. You can create different effects by working wider Fences (as in project #22) or by going either all or half way around the central patch.
Applications: Projects #21, 22, and 23.

To Make Sample Patch With All-Around Fences
With Color A, make a Center-Out Square with Chain-and-Turn method (2 rnds, 20 sts). Add Fences as follows:
Round 1: With Color A, sc into each edge st of the Center-Out Square (3 sc in each corner st). End each rnd with sl st join to first sc. Ch 1, turn now and throughout (28 sts).
Rounds 2 and 3: With Color B, sc in each sc around the Center-Out Square (3 sc in each corner sc), sl st in first sc. Ch 1, turn (44 sts).
Round 4: 1 sc in each sc around, sl st in first sc. Ch 1, turn (44 sts).
A Word to the Wise. From now on increase only on the first and third rounds. However, *always* increase on the last round of the patch.

96

Rounds 5–8: With Color B, sc in each sc around (3 sc into each corner on first and third and last rnd), sl st in first sc (68 sts). Ch 1, turn.

5. Turn square on its point. In same stripe pattern as Center-Out Square, sc a Corner Triangle to each edge (beg each triangle with 1 sc into each of 15 edge sts—sc first 4 rows in Color B, then cont in Color A).

To Make Sample Patch With Half-Way Around Fences

1. Make another sample patch as above. Turn the patch on its point. Then work half way around in rows, which will give you a rectangular shape.

Row 1: With Color B (right side toward you), 1 sc into each of 14 edge sts from one corner to next, 3 sc into the corner sc, 1 sc in each of the next 14 edge sts (the row ends at the corner opposite the one at which you started). Ch1, turn.

Row 2: (Wrong side toward you) make 1 dec in the first 2 sc (see *GENERAL INSTRUCTIONS—Increasing and Decreasing*), sc in each sc to corner in middle of row, 3 sc in corner sc, sc in each sc until you get to last 2 sc, make dec. Ch 1, turn.

Rows 3–8: Rep row 2 (2 × in Color A, 4 × in Color B).

2. Rep rows 1–8 at other side (beg at the same corner but work back and forth around other midpoint).

3. In same stripe pattern, sc a Corner Triangle to each edge.

Note: You can also work Fences half way around a Center-Out Square (without any all-around Fences). For step-by-step details see project #23.

#21 Sawtooth Diamond Square

To successfully translate a design from one craft medium to another takes more than mere copying. The secret is to tap your craft's special strengths and pleasures. In crochet that means taking advantage of the ability to work in any direction, even three-dimensionally—like our adaptation of the popular Sawtooth Diamond pattern. Patches Used: Center-Out Square with Fences and Boxes, Sawtooth Triangles.

Materials/Measurements
Finished Size: Approx. 38 by 38 inches.
Yarn: Phildar "Lenox 084" (wool worsted, 3½-oz.) 3 balls each Hawthorne (Color A) and Teal (Color B).
Hook: Size J.
Gauge: 4 sts = 1 inch, 4 rows/rounds = 1 inch.

Notes
• Mark the spot where you want the points of the Sawtooth Triangles to fall with pins, *before* you attach them to the background. Like basting a hem before sewing, this saves time in the long run.
• To create your own personalized color scheme, let yourself go. Historic examples of Sawtooth patterns give ample evidence that this is truly an anything-goes design. Red and white, silver and red, royal blue and red are fine. Even combinations which might be garish elsewhere, like orange with purple or yellow with kelly green, look just fine here.

Directions
1. With Color A, sc a Center-Out Square using the Chain-and-Turn method (13 inches square, adjust last rnd for 40 sts at each edge).
2. With Color B, (start at any corner, *wrong side toward you*), work 16 sc into the square's edge sts (insert hook into FRONT loops). Ch 1, turn.

3. Make Sawtooth Triangle to fall forward onto square as follows:
Row 1: 1 sc into each of next 8 sc. Ch 1, turn throughout Saw-
tooth Triangle (8 sts).
Row 2: Dec on first 2 sc, 6 sc across (7 sts).
Row 3: 5 sc, sk 1 sc, 1 sc (6 sts).
Row 4: Dec on first 2 sc, 4 sc across (5 sts).
Row 5: 3 sc, sk 1 sc, 1 sc (4 sts).
Row 6: Dec on first 2 sc, 1 sc (3 sts).
Row 7: 1 sc, sk 1 sc, 1 sc (2 sts).
Row 8: 2 sc tog. Ch 1, sl st join triangle tip to background, then sl
st down along the straight edge of the Sawtooth.
4. *Work 8 sc sts into FRONT loops of the Center-Out Square
edge and make another Sawtooth triangle as per rows 1–8 procedure. Rep from *—3 Sawtooth triangles.
5. Sc into Front loops until you get to the corner of the Center-Out
Square. Work 3 sc into the corner. Rep steps 1–5 (3 Sawtooth Triangles each side) 3 × for 12 Sawtooth Triangles all around. End
rnd with sl st join to first sc. Ch 1, turn.
A Word to the Wise. The number of stitches between groups of
triangles is subject to adjustment, depending upon how many
stitches you end up with when you finish the Center-Out Square.
The important thing is not how many stitches you have between
the triangle groups, but that they are evenly spaced all around.
6. (Right side toward you) work sc into each st of same rnd (insert
hook in back loop). Ch 1, turn.
7. Sc in each sc around (3 sc into each corner sc on alternate
rounds—inc on each of last 3 rnds to obtain 80 sts at each edge).
Ch 1, turn and cont for 6 inches (entire piece should be approx. 24
inches square).
8. (Wrong side toward you) switch to Color A, work one rnd into
front loops and add 8 Sawtooth Triangles to each side. Use same
procedures as for first Sawtooth Triangles (these triangles should
begin and end 12 sts from each edge although, as already men-
tioned, this is an adjustable number. What counts is to have the
same number of stitches between each group of triangles.
9. With Color A (right side toward you), work a Corner Triangle to
each edge (beg with approx. 80 ridge sts, cont in sc).
10. With Color B (start at any corner with wrong side toward you),
work one rnd (hook into front loops), adding 8 Sawtooth Triangles
to each side. Make Sawtooth Triangles as before (position them so
that four beg 2 inches from right edge and end 2 inches before the
point of the Color B band; and four beg 2 inches from the left edge
and end 2 inches from the Color B band's point). End the rnd with
a sl st in first sc. Ch 1, turn.
11. (Right side toward you) work into each st of same rnd (insert
hook into back loops). End rnd with sl st join. Ch 1, turn.
12. (Wrong side toward you) sc into each sc around, 3 sc into
each corner sc, end rnd with sl st in first sc. Ch 1, turn. Cont making rnds for 2 inches (inc at corners on alternate rnds). Fasten off.

#22 Barn Raising

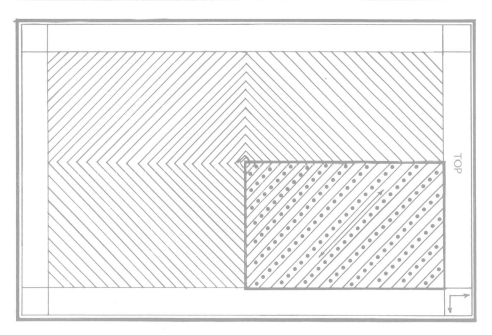

In 19th Century America raising a new barn was a communal activity which inspired a whole category of quilts known as Log Cabins. The stripes in Barn Raising are said to represent lumber laid out on the ground before the business of raising the barn began. This particular "log" variation is so crochetable that it's certain to be as popular with crocheters as with fabric quilters. Our afghan begins with a traditional red center to symbolize the hearth. As a special touch, picot stitches mimic the tiny triangles frequently found in fabric versions of this pattern.
Patches Used: Center-Out Square with Fences and Boxes, Fill-In Squares.

Materials/Measurements
Finished Size: Approx. 47 by 66 inches.
Yarn: Lane Borgosesia "knitaly" (4 wool worsted, 3½-oz.) 7 red (#3793), 6 silver (#991), 4 royal blue (#1415).
Hook: Size I.
Gauge: 7 sts = 2 inches, 9 rows = 2 inches.

Notes
• As you will be working with one very large patch it is especially important to take time regularly to lay your work flat to make sure there's no buckling or pulling to be adjusted with more or fewer stitches.
• The yarn used to make the sample is somewhat finer than most knitting worsteds. Thus even though this afghan is made with 1 large patch, it's light enough to carry around with you. For a larger, bulkier stitch gauge, use the yarn doubled with a size J or K hook. If you do, allow for approximately one third more yarn.
• For a larger quilt, work extra pairs of Fences around the Center-Out Square and extra pairs of Half-Way Around

Fences around each half of the diagonally set square. Be sure to also add picots to the third row of each silver Half-Way Around Fence (2 extras at the beginning and end of each Fence).
• For a different color effect, substitute beige for the silver, or use blue and red for the stripes and a vivid green for the picots.

Directions

1. With red, sc a Center-Out Square (2½ inches square—36 sts).
2. Sc 11 Fences around the Center-Out Square (alternating from silver to red for 6 rnds each). Work 3 sc into the corner sts for the first 2 Fences, then inc on rnds 2, 4 and 6 only. Attach royal blue yarn at the beg of the third rnd of each silver Fence and evenly space picot stitches across each side of the rnd (see *GENERAL INSTRUCTIONS—Bump Stitches*). Space the picots as follows:
Picot Fence 1: Work 1 sc into each of the first 2 sc, *make a picot, sc in each of the next 2 sc, rep from *2 × (carry royal blue yarn along at the back and crochet around it—lock it in on the next rnd). Cont to work 3 picots to each side.
Picot Fences 2–6: Rep above procedure, adding a picot at the beg and end of each side of the square (8 all around)—3 sc in between each of 5 picots on the second Fence; 4 sc between each of 7 picots on the third; 5 sc in between each of 9 picots and 11 picots on the fourth and fifth; 6 sc in between each of 13 picots on the sixth.
A Word to the Wise. Don't worry if the spaces between your picots are not exactly as above. What's important is that the picots added at each side fan out in a V-shaped line.
3. Set the square on its point and with red, sc into the sts along each of 2 sides to beg a Half-Way Around Fence. Start at the corner where you ended the All-Around Fence, work 3 sc into the next corner and cont to the next corner (opposite the one where you began). Ch 1 turn, *make a dec on the first sc, sc in each sc to the midpoint, 3 sc into the corner sc, sc in each sc until you get to the last 2 sts, make another dec. Ch 1. turn Rep from * 4 ×.
4. Make 4 more Fences, alternating red and silver as for the All-Around Fences. Cont the picot pattern on the silver Fences (5 sc between picots) but with just 1 additional picot (at the edge toward the middle).
A Word to the Wise. Count the stitches on the first Half-Way Around Fence row to make sure that you have the same amount at each side. Jot down the number so that you can refer to it when you work the opposite side of the square.
5. Rep steps 3 and 4 around the other half of the square.
6. In the same color sequence as the Fences, sc a Corner Triangle to each side of the Square (8 stripes, beg with silver and end with red). Keep working picots into the third row of the silver stripes, but instead of adding 2 for each stripe, make 2 less (from 9 picots on the first silver stripe to 3 on the last).

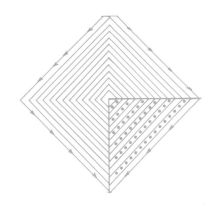

To Make Border

1. With royal blue, sc into the edge sts along the top side (a gauge of 13 sts for every 4 inches should give you a border patch that will lie flat). Ch 1, turn, and rep for 17 additional rows.

A Word to the Wise. Test the border gauge after the first row and add or subtract stitches if necessary. Write down the number of stitches for reference when you work the other border pieces.

2. Rep step 1 at the bottom and side edges.

3. With red, sc a Fill-In Square between the blue border strips (beg with 17 sc into each side edge—adjust number of sts if necessary if square is too tight or too full).

4. With red, sc all around from left to right for a Corded Edge (see *GENERAL INSTRUCTIONS*). Fasten off.

#23 Log Cabin Fences

Fabric quilters classify this Log Cabin pattern as extremely difficult. Happily, the opposite holds true for our crocheted Log Cabin Fences. It's made with repeats of one truly uncomplicated patch made by working a Fence first around one half of a Center-Out Square and next around the opposite half. The bulky yarn provides enough body for your afghan to do double duty as a rug.
Patches Used: Center-Out Squares, and Half-Way Around Fences.

Materials/Measurements
Finished Size: Approx. 65 by 65 inches.
Yarn: Phildar "Kadischa 130" (3 ply acrylic and wool, 1¾ oz.) 12 each Ecru (Color A) and Tabou (Color B); 9 each Maquis (Color C) and Mouflon (Color D); 7 each Cornouaille (Color E), Beige (Color F), and Roux (Color G).
Hook: Size J.
Gauge: 3 sts = 1 inch, 3 rows = 1 inch.
Each patch = 10 inches square.

Notes
• To make a lighter weight quilt with more, but smaller squares, use a regular worsted weight yarn which will produce a square approximately 2 inches smaller.
• For a more rectangular afghan, make 12 squares less and omit the first and last patch when piecing each row. In other words, join 4 patches for each of the 6 rows.
• The only rule for making color changes is that light shades surround one side of an unchanging center and dark shades the other.

Directions
The Log Cabin Patch
Make 36
1. With Color G, make a Center-Out Square with Chain-and-Turn method (3 rnds, 20 sts, 2 inches square).
2. Work rows for Log Cabin Fences as follows.
Row 1: (Right side toward you) with Color F, 1 sc into each of 13 sc along 2 sides of square (including 3 sc in corner sc). Ch 1, turn now and throughout.
Rows 2–4: Rep row 1: (End first Half-Way Around Fence with 19 sts and color switch on last yo).
Row 5: Turn patch so wrong side is toward you. With Color E, 3 sc into Color F edge (4 sts), 1 sc in each of next 4 Color G sts (the side of the Center-Out Square), 3 sc in next Color G sc, 1 sc in each of next 4 Color G sc (the second side of the Center-Out Square), 4 sc in Color F edge.

Rows 6–8: 1 sc into each sc (3 sc into corner sc, end Fence with 25 sts and color switch on last yo).

Row 9: With Color D and right side toward you, 3 sc into Color E edge (4 sts), 1 sc in each of next 19 Color G sc (no corner inc), 4 sc in Color E edge.

Rows 10–12: 1 sc into each sc, (3 sc into corner sc on rnds 10 and 12, end Fence with 31 sts and color switch on last yo).

Row 13: With Color C and wrong side toward you, 3 sc into Color D edge (4 sts), 1 sc in each of next 19 Color E sc, 4 sc in Color D edge.

Rows 14–16: 1 sc in each sc, (3 sc into corner sc on rows 14 and 16, end Fence with 31 sts and color switch).

Row 17: With Color A and right side toward you, 3 sc into Color C edge (4 sts), 1 sc in each of next 31 Color D sts, 4 sc in Color C edge.

Rows 18–20: 1 sc in each sc (3 sc into corner st on rows 18 and 20, end Fence with 43 sts).

Row 21: With Color B and wrong side toward you, 3 sc into Color A edge (4 sts), 1 sc in each of next 31 Color C sts, 4 sc in Color A edge.

Rows 22–24: 1 sc into each sc (3 sc in corner sc on rnds 22 and 24—end Fence 43 sts). Fasten off.

To Join

1. Using assembly diagram as guide now and throughout, ∗line up and join 3 squares with the Fences at the *left and top edge* alternating from Color A to Color B to Color A. Line up and join 3 more squares with the Fences in the Color A-B-A sequence at the top and right edge. Join into 6-square row. Rep from ∗ 3 ×

2. ∗Line up and join 3 squares with the Fences at the *left and top edge* alternating from Color B to Color A to Color B. Line up and join 3 more squares with the Fences at the *top and right edge* in Color B-A-B sequence. Join into 6-square row. Rep from ∗ 3 ×.

3. Join 3 rows (one row made in step 2 sequence sandwiched between two rows made in step 1 sequence) 2 ×.

4. Rep step 3.

5. Join pieced rows at the center (between rows 3 and 4).

A Word to the Wise. When using bulky yarn, take extra care to join patches and weave in yarn ends securely.

To Make Border

Round 1: With Color G (start at any corner), sc into edge sts all around (switch to a gauge of 11 sts for every 4 inches). End rnd with sl st join to first sc. Ch 1, turn.

A Word to the Wise. Lay work flat to check gauge. Adjust gauge for more stitches if border is tight. Adjust for fewer stitches if it ripples.

Round 2: Sc into each sc around (3 sc into each corner st). Ch 1, turn.

Rounds 3–5: Rep rnd 2 (on rnd 4, sk corner incs and switch to Color B). Fasten off.

Round 6: Rep rnd 1. Fasten off.

Granny Patch Five/Center-Out Checkerboard

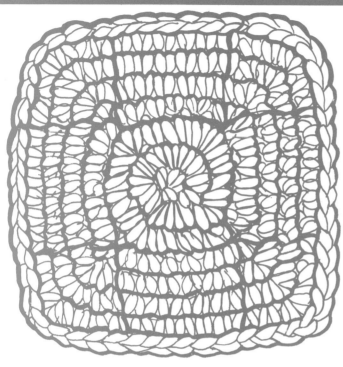

Because Checkerboard Grid patterns like the Nine-Patch are so popular, it's nice to add another method for creating them to your crochet repertoire. Our Granny Patch Checkerboard is a Center-Out Square with the Tapestry Stitch technique used to build up the additional color blocks. The swirling stitch pattern that results adds an interesting dimension which you may well find worth the extra effort and yarn required.
Applications: Project #24, 35 (square 13 border).

To Make Sample Patch

With Color A, sc a Center-Out Square, using the Up-and-Around method. To make this part of the pattern block double layered like the rest, leave an extra long yarn end and carry it along and crochet it as you work the square (2 rounds, 20 sts). Join the last rnd by slip stitching through in Color B, then cont as follows:

Round 1: *Work 3 sc into the first sc (1 each in Colors B-A-B), with Color B, work 1 sc in each of the next 4 sc. Rep from * 3 ×, carrying along and crocheting around yarn not in use. End rnd with sl st join to first sc (sl st through in first sc and sl st through in Color A. Ch 1 (28 sts—6 Color B at each side, 1 Color A at each corner).

Round 2: *With Color A, 3 sc into the Color A sc; with Color B, 1 sc in each of next 6 sc. Rep from * 3 ×. End rnd with sl st in first sc, slip stitching through in Color A. Ch 1. (36 sts all around—6 Color B at each side, 3 Color A at each corner).

Round 3: *With Color A, 1 in first sc, 3 sc in next sc, 1 sc in next sc; with Color B, 1 sc in each of next 6 sc. Rep from * 2 ×. With Color B, 1 sc in next 5 sc. End rnd with sl st in first sc, slip stitching through in Color A (44 sts all around—6 in each Color B side, 5 in Color A corner blocks).

Rounds 4 and 5: Cont in rnd 3 pattern, working Color A sts in A and Color B sts in B, with 3 sc into the corner sts so that the Color A Block ends up with 13 sc (6 at each side and 1 at the corners). **Note:** As you can see, the color blocks at each side of the Center-Out Square always have the same number of stitches whereas the corner blocks are increased by 2 stitches on each round (the 3 single crochets worked into the corner). This principle applies even when additional color blocks are added, as in the next project.

Remember
• When you switch colors, complete the last stitch in the old color with a yo in the next color.
• Always carry and crochet around yarn not in use. Give a gentle tug to the yarn crocheted in at the back, before switching colors again.
• To ensure an even weight for your entire patch, work an extra length of yarn in at the back of the solid color Center-Out Square.

#24

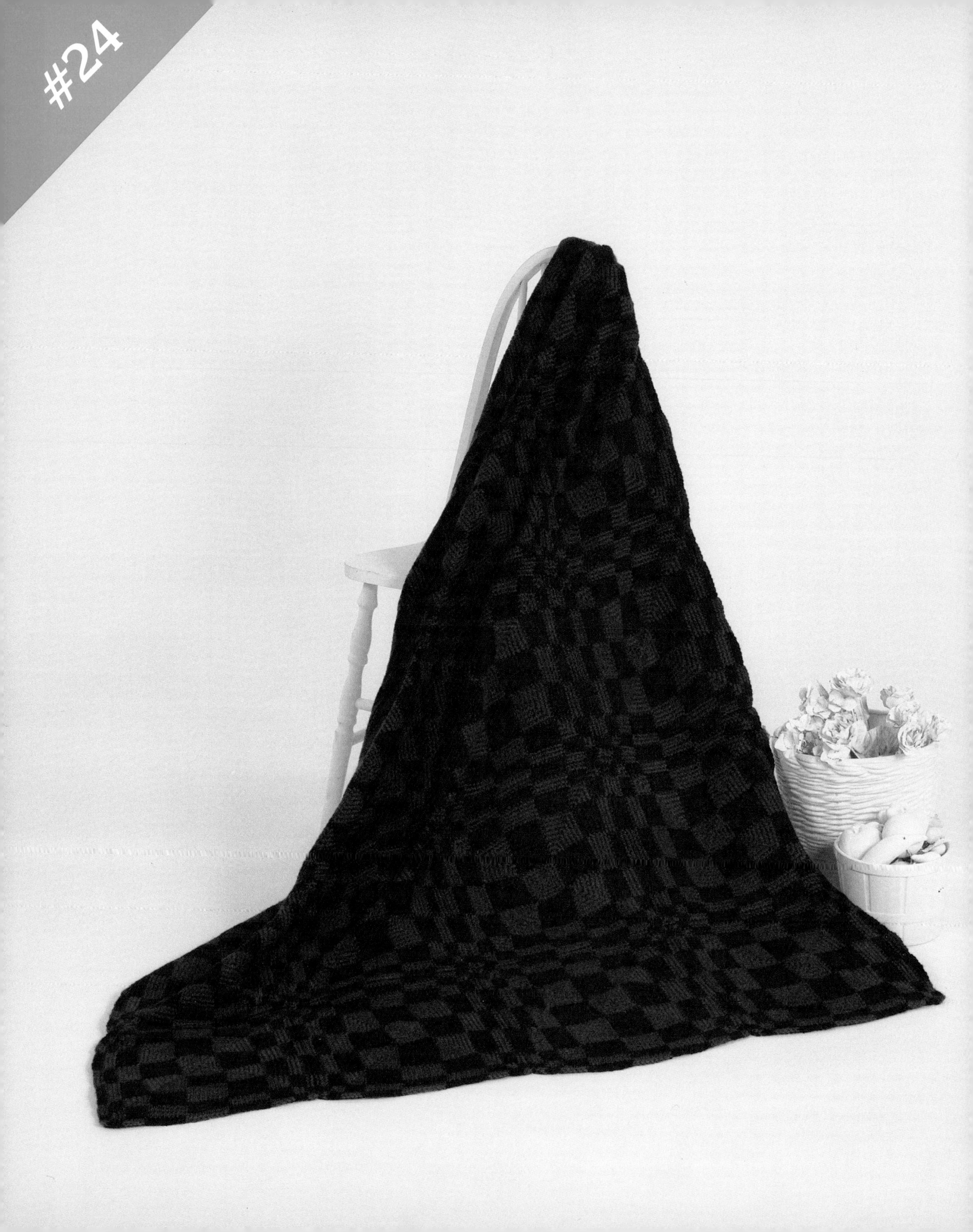

#24 Snail's Trail

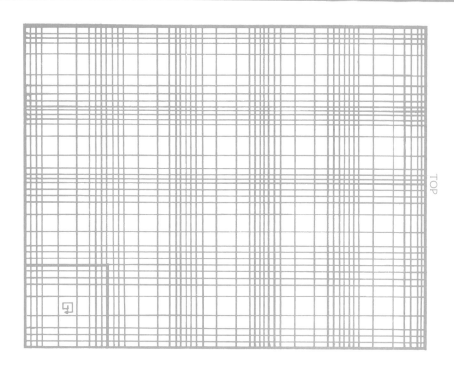

TOP

Materials/Measurements
Finished Size: Approx. 48 ×
60 inches.
Yarn: Phildar "Pegase 206" (4
ply acrylic and worsted, 1¾-oz.)
20 balls each Epice (Color A)
and Tabou (Color B).
Hook: Size I.
Gauge: 4 sts = 1 inch,
4 rounds = 1 inch.
Each pattern square = 12
inches.

Notes
• Remember to end your
rounds with a sl st into the first
single crochet made, skipping
the sl st join.
• Don't forget to carry and crochet around the yarn not in use.
• Check out the fourth square
in the Sampler (project #35)
for a row-by-row version of the
Snail's Trail pattern.
• The white with blue, red or
gold combinations often used
in old coverlets would make ex-
cellent color alternatives for this
project.

This afghan could easily have
been inspired by a modern
painting, but is in fact adapted
from an 18th century woven
coverlet. The graduated sizes of
the Checkerboards and the
swirling stitch pattern emphasize the woven effect. The iden-
tical patches dovetail neatly to
form the self-bordered Snail's
Trail.
Patches Used: Center-Out
Checkerboard Squares.

Directions
The Snail's Trail Square
Make 20
1. With Color A, sc a Center-
Out Square (approx. 2½ inches,
36 sts all around). Use the Up-
and-Around Method. Carry and
crochet around an extra layer of
yarn as for the sample Center-
Out Checkerboard. When you
join last rnd, sl st through in
Color B. Ch 1.
2. Work the first set of Checkerboard blocks as for the sample Center-Out Checkerboard
Patch but with 9 sts at each
side for 9 rnds (beg with a
Color B-A-B inc in first sc, 7 sc
in Color B and rep 3 × to end
of rnd; inc the corners to 19
sts).

3. Work the 2nd set of Checkerboards for 5 rnds as follows:
Round 1: With Color B, 1 sc in each of 8 sc; with Colors B-A-B, 3 sc in next sc; with Color B, 1 sc in each of next 8 sc, with Color A, 1 sc in each of next 9 sc. Rep from * 2 ×. Cont to end of rnd with 9 sc in Color B, 9 sc in Color A, 3 sc into corner (B-A-B), 9 sc in Color A, 8 sc in Color B, sl st in first sc (slip stitching through in Color A).
Rounds 2–5: With Color B, sc in all Color B sc (9 sts each side); with Color A sc in all Color A sc (3 sc in each corner so that Color A block grows from 1 to 9 sts). End rnd 5 by slip stitching through in Color A. Ch 1 for the next set of Checkerboards.
4. Work 3rd set of Checkerboard blocks for 3 rnds as follows:
Round 1: *With Color A, 1 sc into each of 9 Color B sc; with Color B, 1 sc in each of next 4 Color A sc; with Colors B-A-B, 3 sc in next sc (the corner); with Color B, 1 sc in each of next 4 Color A sc; with Color B, 1 sc in each of next 9 Color A sc; with Color A, 1 sc in each of next 9 Color B sc. Rep from * 2 ×. Cont to end of rnd with 9 sc in Color A, 9 sc in Color B, 3 sc in corner sc in Colors B-A-B, 9 sc in Color B, 9 sc in Color A, 8 sc in Color B. End rnd with sl st in first sc. Ch 1.
Rounds 2 and 3: Cont in above pattern, working 3 sc into each corner sc of the little Color A blocks so that they grow to 7 st (3 at each side). At the end of rnd 3, sl st through in Color B. Ch 1 for the next set of Checkerboards.
5. Work a final set of Checkerboard blocks for 2 rnds as follows:
*With Color B, 1 sc into each of 9 Color A sc; with Color A, 1 sc in each of next 5 Color B sc; with Color B, 1 sc in each of next 3 sc; with Colors B-A-B, 3 sc in next sc (the corner); with Color B, 1 sc in each of next 3 sc; with Color A, 1 sc in each of next 5 sc; with Color B, 1 sc in each of next 9 Color A sc. Rep from * 2 ×. Cont to end of rnd with 9 sc in Color B, 5 sc in Color A, 3 sc in Color B, 3 into corner in Colors B-A-B, 3 sc in Color B, 5 sc in Color A, 9 sc in Color B, 8 sc in Color A. End rnd with sl st join. Fasten off.

To Join
1. Join squares into five 4-unit rows.
2. Join the rows.

Granny Patch Six/Circle

Most patterns are made with straight edged units. With the Circle the adventurous crocheter's horizon expands to include a whole range of out-of-the-ordinary quilt designs. While circular motifs can be crocheted to any size, for our purpose they're most effective when kept small, with a diameter not exceeding four inches. Applications: Projects #25 and 26.

To Make Sample Patch

Make a loosened slip knot (see *GRANNY PATCHES AND PROJECTS* introductory section), ch 1, work 5 sc into the slip knot (around the double layer of yarn), sl st join to first sc to form ring. Ch 1 (6 sts).

Round 1: 2 sc in each of 5 sc, 1 sc in last sc of rnd. End rnd with sl st join to first sc. Ch 1 (12 sts).

Round 2: 2 sc into each sc, sl st in first sc. Ch 1 (24 sts).

Round 3: 2 sc into first sc, *1 sc in next sc, 2 sc into next sc, rep from * until 1 sc is left. Work 1 sc into last sc, sl st in first sc. Ch 1 (36 sts).

Round 4: Sc into each sc around, sl st in first sc (36 sts). Fasten off.

Remember

• To end rounds for single crocheted circles, always slip stitch join to the first single crochet, skipping the join of the previous round.
• The number of stitches with which to begin a Circle can be varied as needed (see project #26).

#25

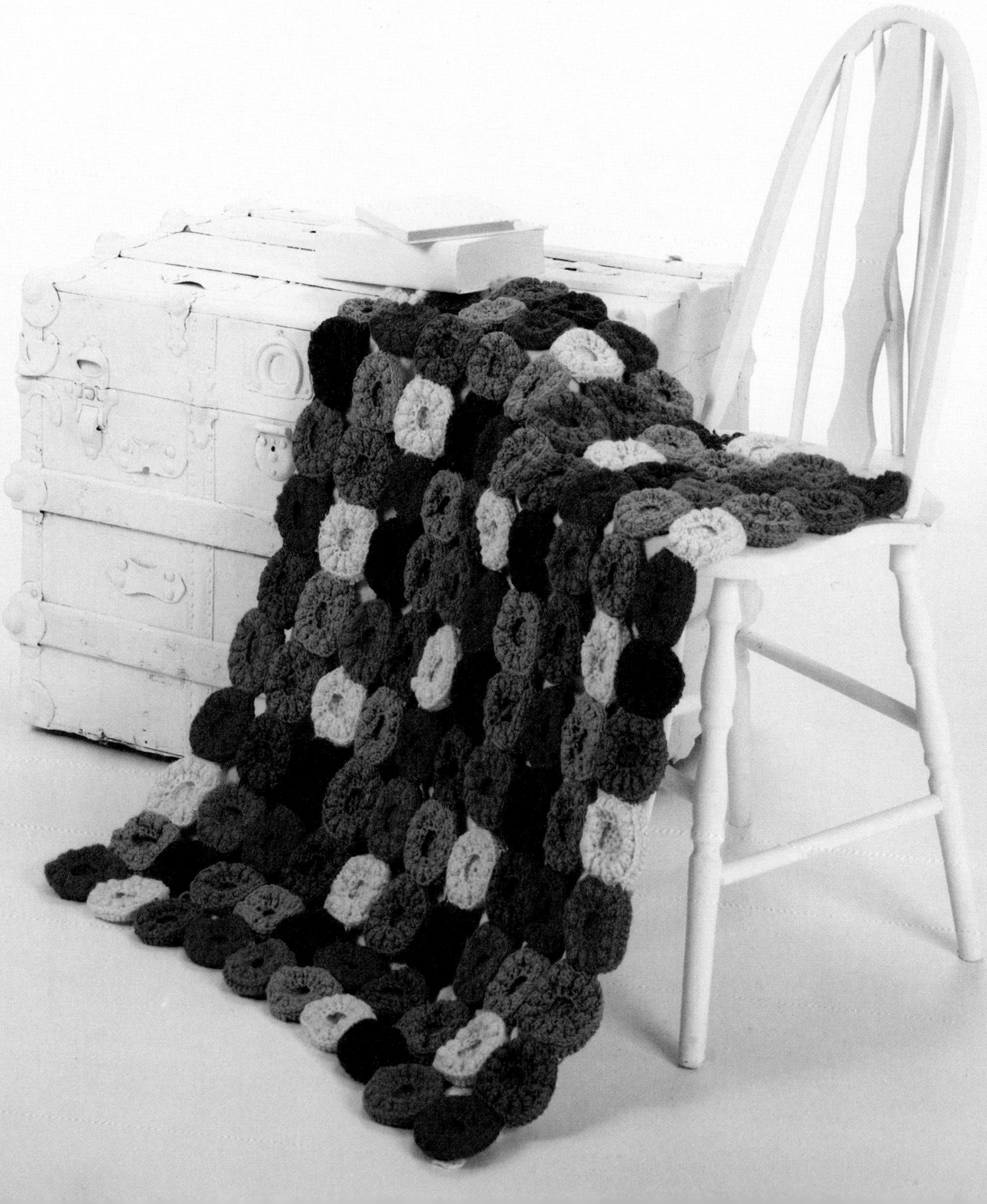

#25 Yo-Yos

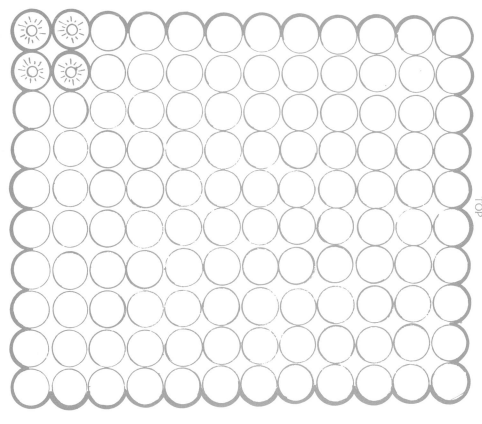

Yo-Yos, also known as Fabric Rosettes and Puffballs, came into prominence during the 1920s. They were made by running a basting stitch around the edge of a flat round fabric patch, then pulling the thread tight to form a puffy little flower. Our crochet adaptation also starts with a flat Circle which is then puffed and shaped with several rounds of sharp increases and decreases. Patches Used: Circles.

Materials/Measurements

Finished Size: Approx. 32 by 42 inches.

Yarn: Phildar "Lenox 084" (wool worsted, 3½-oz.) 4 balls Flame (Color A), 3 balls each Ecru (Color B), Teal (Color C), Baroque (Color D), Celestial (Color E), 2 balls each Titian (Color G) and Hawthorne (Color F).

Hook: Size J.

Gauge: 3 sts = 1 inch, 3 rounds = 3 inches. Each yo-yo = 3½–inches in diameter.

Notes

• Although this is a good scrap yarn project, avoid bulky yarns which will give you a top-heavy project. Whatever yarn you use, join all units firmly but without pulling the patches out of shape.

• The colors in the sample quilt were randomly arranged and any combination of three to ten or even more colors would work.

• For a larger afghan with a more controlled color format, make 130 Yo-Yos (82 in a dark color and 48 in a light color). Make 5 rows with 10 dark units.

Make 8 rows with 1 dark alternating with 2 light units (beg and end with dark). Join the multi-color rows into pairs, then sandwich a pair of multi-color rows between two rows with all dark colors.

Directions

The Yo-Yo

Make 120: 21 Color A, 18 each Color B and Color E, 17 Color C, 16 Color D, 15 each Color G and Color F.

1. Sc a Circle as per *Granny Patch Six—To Make Sample Patch,* (Approx 3½-inches in diameter—36 sts). Ch 1.

2. To begin the puff effect make a raised ridge around the circle by single crocheting around the stitch stem (the little bars beneath the chain into which you usually insert your hook). End rnd with sl st join. Ch 1.

A Word to the Wise. To work around the bars beneath the chain, insert the hook from front to back (to the right of the bars), then around the back and through to the front (to the left of the bars).

3. *3 sc in first sc, 2 sc in the next sc, 1 sc in next sc. Rep from * to end of rnd (the increases will create a ruffle).

4. To pull in the "puff" *1 sc, sk 5, rep from * to end of rnd. Fasten off, leaving 6-inch length.

5. Thread the yarn end through an embroidery needle. Weave the threaded needle in and out of the edge sts of the "puff". Pull the yarn to tighten the ring, leaving a 1-inch opening.

To Join Yo-Yos

1. Assemble Yo-Yos as in diagram—12 rows each with 10 patches. (This is a random pattern. See Notes for other color arrangements).

2. Join yo-yos weaving yarn in and out through the inside. *Do not cut ends short and rely on a knot to hold the join.* These patches require solid connections.

#26 Nosegays

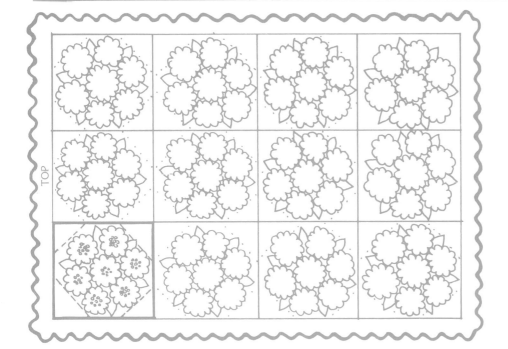

Whereas with patchwork you create a fabric as you piece the pattern together, with Appliqué you decorate a background fabric with a "laid-on" design. In the 19th century quilt which inspired our Nosegays the flowers were sewn to a solid white fabric. In our crocheted version the background is pieced around richly textured Nosegays. Patches Used: Circles, Corner Triangles and Fill-In Squares.

Materials/Measurements
Finished Size: Approx. 37 by 61 inches.
Yarn: Bernat Sesame "4" (wool knitting worsted, 3½-oz.) 8 oyster white, 2 each geranium red, arbutus pink, light tap gold, 1 moss green.
Hook: Size I.
Gauge: 7 sts = 2 inches, 4 rows = 1 inch.
Individual Nosegays = Approx. 3¼ inches in diameter.
Finished Nosegay unit = Approx. 11 by 14 inches.
Special Abbreviation: MC = color used for Nosegay flowers.

Notes
• See *GENERAL INSTRUCTIONS—Bump Stitches,* for how to make picots.
• In a project like this, where a circular motif ends up with straight edges, instructions for the number of stitches to work between the squaring off units are subject to adjustments. The important thing is to make notes of everything you do when you make the first Nosegay unit and to then be absolutely consistent from patch to patch.
• Before you make the shell border, review the one used in project #33, which would look equally lovely here. This can be made all in white like the single shell pictured here.

• The sample uses the same colors for each group of flowers. Feel free to "plant" your garden to suit your color preferences, with each group of Nosegays different or with fantasy instead of realistic colors.

Directions

The Nosegay Flowers

Make 84—24 each white with red centers, red with gold centers, gold with pink centers and 12 pink with gold centers.

With the color of the Nosegay center, work 7 sc into a loosened slip knot (see *GRANNY PATCHES AND PROJECTS* introductory section), insert hook in first sc to form 8 st circle, slip stitching through in the MC. Ch 1 (8 sts).

Round 1: 1 picot and 1 sc into each of 7 sc (sc and picot all in 1 st), 1 picot into the last sc. End rnd with sl st in first sc. Ch 1 (16 sts including 8 picots all around).

Round 2: *Work 1 sc in the ch behind the picot (hold the picot forward to lock in place), 2 sc in the next sc. Rep from *6×. Work 2 sc into the sc after the last picot. End rnd with sl st in first sc. Ch 1 (24 sts).

Round 3: 1 sc and 1 picot into first sc (sc and picot all in one st), 1 sc in next sc, *1 picot and 1 sc in next sc, 1 sc in next sc. Rep from *10×. Work 1 picot and 1 sc in next sc, sl st in first sc. Ch 1. (12 picots made, 36 sts all around).

Round 4: 1 sc into each of the 3 sc between the first 11 picots, 1 sc in the next 2 sc. End rnd with sl st in first sc. (36 sts). Fasten off.

To Join Nosegays and Add Leaves

1. Arrange 6 patches around 1 central patch. Join the encircling patches to the center patch (attach along 6 edge sts containing 2 picots).

2. Join the Nosegay patches at each side to form one 7-patch Nosegay unit (attach once again along 6 sts with 2 picots).

A Word to the Wise. Don't bother to match up yarn when you join the patches. Instead, use green to do it all. Any little bits of this that will show through will tie in nicely with the leaves you'll be adding.

3. With green, sc 6 Fill-In Squares (5 rows each) between each of 2 Nosegays. Beg with 5 sc into the edge sts of one Nosegay (parallel with 2 picots), then work 5 sc up along the edge of the adjoining Nosegay.

4. When you get to the point of the Fill-In Square leaf, do not fasten off. Instead, add a "vein" to the surface of the leaf by working 5 sl sts from the leaf point to the base. Fasten off (bring yarn end to back and leave a 6-inch length hanging in place).

5. Rep steps 3 and 4 between the other Nosegays (5× for 6 leaves).

To Fill In White Background

1. With white, sc a Corner Triangle to the edges of 2 Nosegays. Beg and end at the midpoint of each with 8 sc into the edge sts of the first Nosegay, ch 5, stretch the ch-5 across the back of the leaf, 8 sc in the edge sts of the adjoining Nosegay. Ch 1, turn, cont until the triangle is complete. Rep from * 3× for a rectangular form.

A Word to the Wise. Check your Corner Triangle to make sure it squares off the corner without pulling or rippling. Go back and adjust the number of stitches as needed.

2. Rep step 1 at the other 3 corners.

3. With white (start anywhere), sc all around. End rnd with a sl st join to first sc. Turn and rep 4×.

A Word to the Wise. When squaring off circular units, there's bound to be some unevenness. To adjust for this, work in half double crochet wherever the single crochet edge dips. Also, increase or decrease the number of stitches worked wherever there's any pulling or rippling.

To Join Finished Nosegay Units

1. Join Nosegay rectangles into 4 rows containing 3 rectangles each, then join the rows.

2. Edge the entire quilt with shell sts (*1 sc into first sc, sk 2 sts, 5 dc in next sc, sk 2 sts. Rep from * all around). When you're about 5 inches from the corner, count the remaining sts and inc or dec as needed to work a shell in the corner (see *GENERAL INSTRUCTIONS—Shell Edges*).

Granny Patch Seven/Octagon

The octagon completes your education in geometric shapes built from a circular foundation. Corner Triangles added to four of the Octagon's eight sides make piecing a cinch. Both solid-color and multi-colored Octagons work and look best if you chain one and turn at the end of each round.
Application: Projects #27 and 28.

To Make Sample Solid Color Octagon Patch
Make a loosened slip knot (see *GRANNY PATCHES AND PROJECTS introductory section*), ch 1, work 5 sc into the slip knot (around the double layer of yarn), sl st the last sc to the first sc to form a ring. Ch 1. (6 sts)

Round 1: 2 sc into each sc, sl st in first sc to join. Ch 1, turn (12 sts).

Round 2: (Wrong side toward you on this and all even numbered rnds) rep rnd 1 (24 sts).

Round 3: 1 sc in each of 23 sc. End rnd with the combination sc/sl st join introduced in Granny Patch Two (insert hook on last inc of rnd insert hook, yo and pull through so that 2 lps remain, then in first sc, sl st through 2 lps). Ch 1, turn (24 sts).

Round 4: 2 sc into first sc *1 sc in each of next 2 sc, 2 sc in next sc. Rep from * 6×, 1 sc in next sc, sc/sl st join next sc to first sc as in rnd 3. Ch 1, turn, (32 sts).

Round 5: 2 sc in first sc, *1 sc in each of next 3 sc, 2 sc in next sc. Rep from *6×, 1 sc in each of next 2 sc. Sc/sl st next sc to first sc as in rnd 3. Ch 1, turn (40 sts).

Note: By now you can clearly see your corners so that counting stitches becomes unnecessary.

Round 6: 2 sc in first sc, *1 sc in each of next 4 sc, 2 sc in next sc, rep from * 6 ×, 1 sc in each of next 3 sc. Sc/sl st next sc to first sc as in rnd 3. Ch 1 (48 sts). Fasten off.

To make a larger Octagon, continue in above pattern of working 2 increases into each corner. The number of stitches between the corners increase by 1 on each round—5 in between increases on round 7, 6 on round 8 and so forth. For a very large patch, work an occasional round with a decrease in between corners in order to prevent rippling.

To Make Multi-Colored Octagon Patch

With Color A, form a circle (6 sts) as for the Solid-Color Patch.

Rounds 1 and 2: Work as for Solid-Color patch (24 sts).

Round 3: (Right side toward you) attach Color B into any st along edge, *work 1 sc into each of 3 sc, switch to Color A and work 1 sc in each of next 3 sts. Rep around until you have 7 alternating color segments. With Color A, work 1 sc in each of last 2 sc. End rnd with same combination sc/sl st join used in previous patch and Granny Patch 2 (work first half of sc inc, insert hook into next sc and again into first (Color B) sc, sl st through 2 lps). Ch 1, turn. (You've worked 24 stitches without increasing, like round 4 in the previous patch, but in alternating colors).

Round 4: In color pattern established on previous rnd (beg with A on this and all rnds with wrong side toward you), sc around (2 sc into the first and last sc for each of first 7 color segment so that each segment has 5 sts). On last segment, work 2 sc into the first sc, 1 sc in each of next 4 sc. End rnd with sc/sl st join as on previous rnd. Ch 1, turn (40 sts).

Round 5: In same color pattern, sc around (do not inc). End rnd with sc/sl st join as before. Ch 1, turn (40 sts).

Rounds 6 and 7: Rep rnds 4 and 5, for these and any additional rnds (see project #28 for adjusting the increases for a large patch with bulky yarn).

Remember

• To switch colors, complete the last stitch of the old color with a yo in the next color.

• Carry along and crochet around the yarn not being used. And don't forget to give a little tug at the color you've been carrying along before switching colors.

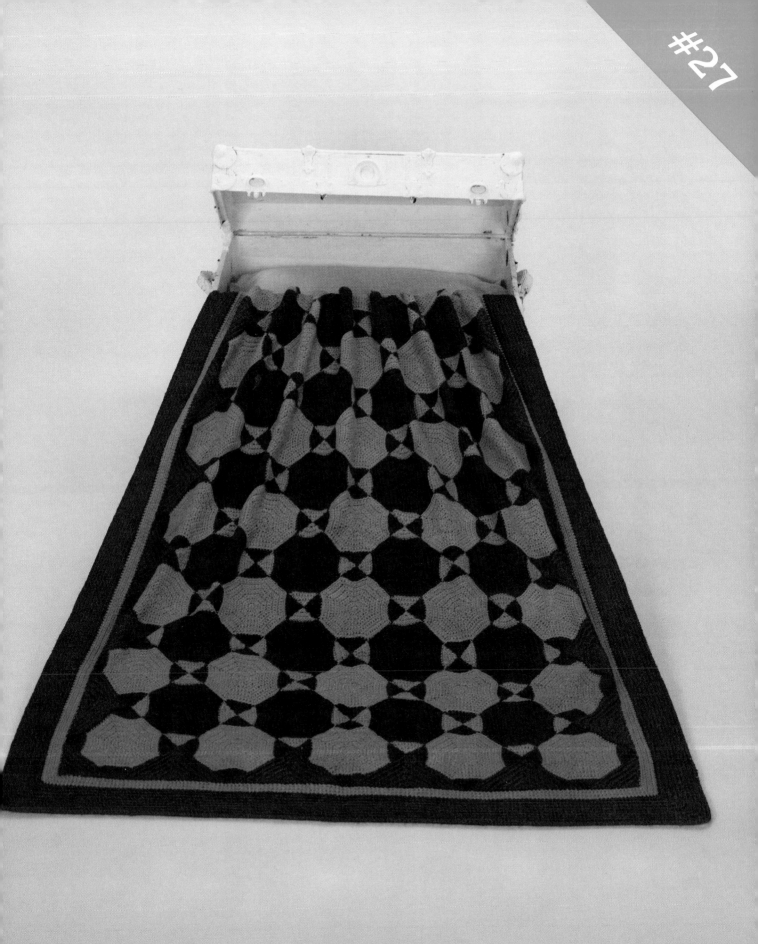

#27 Melon Patch

Here's what you might call the ultimate example of how a simple reversal of colors can create a spectacular all-over pattern from a single design unit—in this case, an Octagon squared out with Corner Triangles. Melon Patch takes its name and color scheme from a cotton quilt made in Pennsylvania in the last quarter of the 19th century.
Patches Used: Solid Center-Out Octagons, Fill-In and Corner Triangles.

Materials/Measurements
Finished Size: Approx. 53 by 69 inches.
Yarn: Scheepjeswol Superwash Zermatt (wool worsted, 1¾-oz.) 13 each; gold (#4858) and red (#4845), 11 green (#4805).
Hook: Size I.
Gauge: 7 sts = 2 inches, 4 rounds = 1 inch.
Each Octagon = 6½ inch square.

Notes
• If your Octagons don't lie completely flat after the 6th round, make 1 decrease between corners for one round. Repeat if necessary.
• Remember you can work the Fill-In and Corner Triangles without breaking off yarn by slip stitching from the end of one patch to the beginning of the next.
• Check out *Graph Pattern Projects* for an Octagon worked in rows instead of from the center out.

Directions
The Center-Out Octagons
Make 35 with gold centers and green corners, 24 with green centers and gold corners.
1. Follow instructions for the Sample Solid Color Octagon Patch that precedes this project. Work 10 rnds which will give you 80 sts all around each patch.

2. Sc a green Corner triangle to every other edge of a gold Octagon and a gold Corner triangle to every other edge of a green Octagon (beg with 11 sc into each edge).

3. Assemble and join patches into 9 rows in alternating colors (2 each with 3, 5 and 7 patches, 3 each with 9 patches—beg and end each row with a gold Octagon with green corners.

4. Join the pieced rows to match the assembly diagram.

5. Join a gold Octagon with green corners to the middle of each 3-patch row.

To Fill In the Edges and Make Border

1. With red, ridge st 20 Fill-In Triangles in between the Octagons, (4 each at the top and bottom, 6 at each side. Beg each Fill-In with 25 sc into each Octagon edge.

2. With red, ridge st a Corner Triangle to each corner gold/green Octagon square. Once again, beg each triangle with 25 sc into the edge.

3. With gold (start anywhere, with right side toward you), sc into the edge sts all around (use a gauge of 13 sts for every 4 inches for a border that will lie flat). End the rnd with a sl st in the first sc. Ch 1, turn.

4. Sc into each sc around (3 sc into each corner sc). End rnd with sl st in the first sc. Ch 1, turn.

5. Rep steps 3 and 4 to cont border (4 rnds gold sc, 18 rnds red ridge st). Fasten off.

#28 Windmill Blades

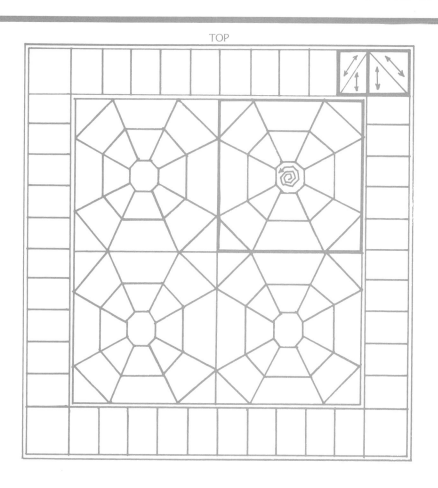

TOP

Windmill Blades is another member of the Log Cabin family of patterns. Our crocheted Windmills consist of four large multi-colored Octagons, squared off with Corner Triangles. When pieced, the red tips of the Corner Triangles form the center of a striking secondary pattern. The brilliantly striped border pushes the central design forward. We made our sample with bulky yarn which not only works up fast but has enough body to be used as a hanging or rug. Patches Used: Multi-Color Octagons, Sawtooth and Across Triangle Squares.

Materials/Measurements
Finished Size: Approx. 48 by 48 inches.
Yarn: Phildar "Kadischa 130" (3 ply acrylic and wool, 1¾-oz.—extra thick yarn) 14 Prusse (Color A). 5 each Tourterelle (Color B) and Bison (Color C). 4 Eglantine (Color D), 3 Alouette (Color E), 2 each Tabou (Color F) and Rouge Color (G).
Hook: Size J.
Gauge: 5 sts = 2 inches, 3 rows = 1 inch.
Each Windmill = 20 inches square.

Notes
• Be sure to carry and crochet around yarn not being used. Give a gentle tug to the carried yarn before you use it again. And remember that the last stitch of each round is joined to the first with a combination single crochet slip stitch (hook into last sc and again in first sc, sl st through 2 lps).
• This is a good time to re-read *GENERAL INSTRUCTIONS—Tapestry Stitch Color Changes* which describes the Stretch-in-Back Method for keeping carried yarn show-through to a minimum.

• If you change the color format, bear in mind that this pattern is most dramatic if one set of "blades" is dark and the other bright. Also remember to plan for a few stripes to run through all the color segments as they do in the sample.

127

Directions

1. Make 4 Octagons following the instructions in *Granny Patch Seven—To Make Multi-Color Octagon Patch* for 27 rnds. Work the first 2 rnds (the circle) in Color G without turning at the end of each rnd. Follow the chart below for color and inc pattern for rnds 3–27. Because the Octagons are large and the yarn thick, you inc on every third instead of every second rnd to prevent rippling.

Color and Increase Sequence for Alternating Windmill Segments
The colors are listed in the order in which they are worked to the Color G center. The asterisks mark the rounds on which an increase should be made at the beginning and end of each segment.

		Alternating	Segments
Round	1	Color B	Color A
Round	2	Color B	Color A
Round	3	Color D	Color A
*Round	4	Color D	Color A
Round	5	Color B	Color A
*Round	6	Color B	Color A
Round	7	Color C	Color C
Round	8	Color C	Color C
*Round	9	Color B	Color A
Round	10	Color B	Color A
Round	11	Color B	Color A
*Round	12	Color B	Color A
Round	13	Color D	Color A
Round	14	Color D	Color A
*Round	15	Color F	Color F
Round	16	Color F	Color F
Round	17	Color F	Color A
*Round	18	Color F	Color A
Round	19	Color F	Color A
Round	20	Color F	Color A
*Round	21	Color F	Color A
Round	22	Color F	Color A
Round	23	Color D	Color A
*Round	24	Color D	Color A
*Round	25	Color C	Color C

2. Sc a Corner Triangle to every other segment (the ones in which Color A predominates). With Color A, sc into each of the 21 edge sts. When you get down to 7 sts, switch to red to complete the triangle.

3. Line up and join the squared off Octagon squares so that the Corner Triangles form a square.

Strip Border

Make 4 strips of Sawtooth and Across Triangle Squares—2 with 10 patches and 2 with 12 patches

With Color C, ch 11.

1. Sc 2 rows each in Colors C and B, dec 1 st at the right edge of each row.

2. Sc the Across triangle to the Sawtooth edge (beg with Color G and work 1 sc into each of 13 edge sts, cont for 2 rows each in Colors G, E and F (switch to Color C to beg next Sawtooth unit).

3. With Color C, work 1 sc in each of 11 sts along the top edge of the first Sawtooth Triangle and Across. Ch 1, turn.

4. Rep steps 1–3 to complete a 10-unit strip.

5. Rep steps 1–3 for another 10-unit and two 12-unit strips.

6. With a size smaller hook, join a 10-unit strip to the top and bottom edges, then join a 12-unit strip to each side edge. To join, place the border strip and the afghan together with the right side facing out and sc through both edges. Leave the corner units unattached and sew join from the back later.

7. With Color A, (stick with the smaller hook), sc into the edge sts all around (3 sc into each corner st). End rnd with sl st join. Fasten off.

8. (Optional) To hang the afghan, make 2 casings in Color A and join to the top and bottom of the border, just below and above the edging rounds. (See GENERAL INSTRUCTIONS—How To Make Casings for Hanging Afghans).

For a more rectangular afghan,
make 24 pattern squares
for 6 rows with 4 Windmills in
each. For an afghan with this
many units, switch to a lighter
weight yarn and smaller hook
which will produce smaller design units.

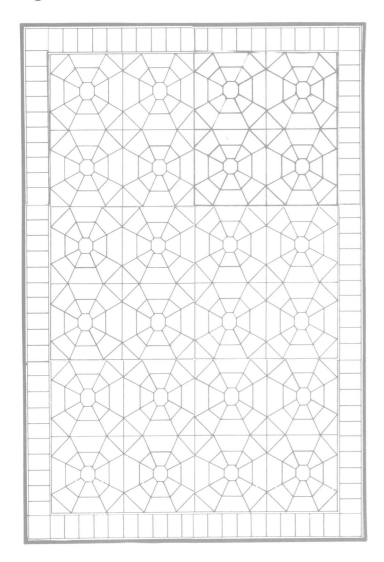

Stuffed
Patches
and

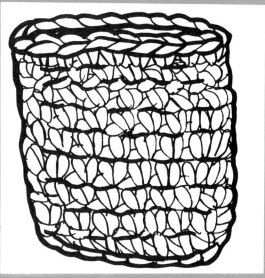

Projects

Here's a unique and enjoyable crochet method de-
vised especially for this
book. It's a cross between
crocheting in rows and
rounds, beginning with one
and continuing with the
other. The way this works
is that you start with a
chain, as for a Plain Patch,
but when you crochet back
along the base chain you
continue around the other
side. The little pouch thus
created is stuffed and
sealed with each color
change.

Stuffed Patch/Stuffed Pouch Strip

Stuffed patches are always crocheted in strips. They can be rectangular as well as square, but they must be worked in accordance with a pre-planned color chart that encompasses the overall pattern. That includes the border. Stuffed patches look particularly nice and work up extra fast with the quilt stitch introduced in *GENERAL INSTRUCTIONS*. However, with yarn that tends to create a loose texture, single crochet is preferable as it keeps the stuffing from showing through.

Applications: Projects #29 and 30.

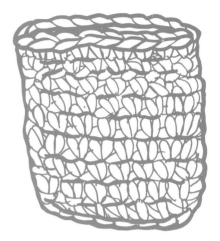

To Make Sample Patch

With Color A, ch 10.

Round 1: Quilt st in 2nd ch from hook and in each of next 8 chs (insert hook, yo and through 1 lp, yo again and through remaining lps). *Do not turn to go back.* Instead, quilt st in the back lp of 8th ch (the other side of the ch) and in each of the next 8 chs. End rnd with sl st join to first st (you've made 18 sts, 9 at the front and 9 at the back). Ch 2.

Round 2: Quilt st in each st around, sl st join to the first st of rnd. Ch 2.

Rounds 3–8: Rep rnd 2. Switch to Color B at end of rnd 8 and insert stuffing.

Round 9: (This round seals the just completed and stuffed pouch and begins next patch). Work a quilt st through each of 9 sts *at the front and back of the pouch* (beg each st by inserting hook through the back loop of a st at the front *and* through the front loop of a st at the back). Turn the sealed pouch so that the back is toward you and work a quilt st into each of the 7 lps left exposed when you sealed the first pouch. End rnd with sl st join to first st. Ch 2.

Rounds 10–16: Rep rnds 2–8.

Round 17: Rep rnd 9 to cont the strip.

Remember

• The easiest way to enlarge a stuffed pattern is to add a few stitches and rows to each pouch. For best results, don't make your pouches too big.

• Always make a sample pouch and stuff it. If the stuffing shows through work in single crochet (you'll need at least a stitch more per row and a row more per pouch to obtain the same sized unit).

• You can crochet any patch which can be divided into equal color grids in this double-layered fashion, for example, the patches in projects #3, 8, 9 and 23. Bear in mind that the color grid from which you work encompasses the overall afghan pattern (including the border). In short, the stuffed pouch strips run from the bottom of the pieced pattern blocks to the top. Another important factor to consider is that regular pattern blocks expand when translated into Stuffed Pouch Strips.

#29 Sunshine and Shadows

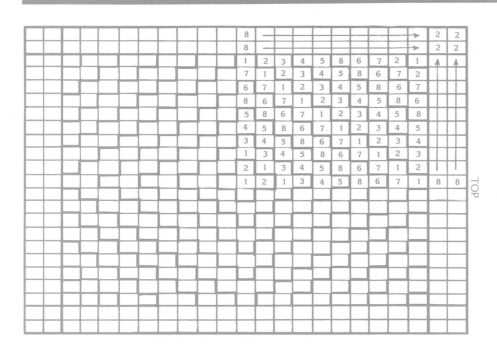

Sunshine and Shadows, also known as Grandma's Dream, is a shining example of the Amish quilters' ability to impart mood and meaning to geometric shapes. It is also an ideal project for familiarizing yourself with the Stuffed Pouch Strip. It's relaxing to make, stunning to look at . . . a true heirloom when finished.
Patches Used: Stuffed Pouch Strip.

Materials/Measurements
Finished Size: 57 × 61 inches.
Yarn: Bernat Sesame "4" (wool worsted weight, 3½-oz.), 9 moss green, 4 arbutus pink, 3 each terra cotta, burgundy, maroon heather, shadow blue, pale olive, light tap gold.
Stuffing: 1 package Poly-Fil® quilt batting.
Hook: Size I.
Gauge: 9 quilt sts = 3 inches, 8 rounds = 3 inches.
Each stuffed module = 3 inches by 3¼ inches.

Notes
• As you complete strips lay them next to each other to make sure that everything lines up and conforms to the chart.
• To work in single crochet instead of quilt stitch, sc 10 sts per rnd and 10 rnds per pouch.
• For a larger, more rectangular design, chain 12 for 11 quilt stitches at each side and crochet 11 rounds per module.
• To deepen the "Shadows" in your design, add deep and medium purple, crimson and deep blue around a dark brown center. For more emphasis on the "Sunshine" colors, work gold, white, pale blue and three shades of red around an orange center.

Directions

1. Quilt st 19 Stuffed Pouch Strips, with 19 pouches for each unit. Work like the sample patch in the previous section, in colors indicated in the color and assembly chart.

A Word to the Wise. Stop occasionally to count your stitches and rounds (18 sts each rnd, 8 rnds each pouch) to make sure all your stuffed color blocks are the same size and will line up when joined.

2. Sew join the finished units. For a seamless join, match the yarn to each pouch edge. Before you switch to a new color, push the needle through the inside of the pouches and pull the yarn through to the point where you'll use it again.

3. (Optional) with moss green, make 2 casings to hang quilt (see *GENERAL INSTRUCTIONS*) and sew to top and bottom border.

Color Code for Sunshine and Shadows Pattern Chart

1 = terra cotta
2 = arbutus pink
3 = burgundy
4 = maroon heather
5 = shadow blue
6 = pale olive
7 = light tap gold
8 = moss green

#30 Courthouse Steps

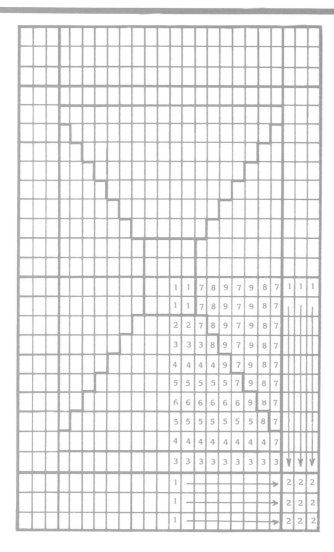

Courthouse Steps is another variation on the Log Cabin theme. Light and dark colors are evenly paired at opposite sides of a central block to form a giant "step." Because the steps are built with Stuffed Pouch strips you can carry the work with you wherever you go just as you would an afghan made with multiple pattern blocks.

Patches Used: Stuffed Pouch Strips.

Notes

• For a more traditional Log Cabin color scheme, start with a red center. As for the colors at either side of the center pouch, anything goes ... as long as you put the darker, deeper colors on one side and the lighter ones on the other.

• If you prefer to use the quilt stitch (see sample Stuffed Pouch Strip and last project), use a size smaller hook for a denser fabric.

• You might want to follow up this stuffed afghan with a stuffed version of the #23 Log Cabin pattern. The pattern patches can be easily divided into a grid (7 squares across, 7 down). Eliminate the border and use only half the pattern blocks because they expand as stuffed patches.

Materials/Measurements

Finished Size: Approx. 57½ by 69 inches.

Yarn: Scheepjeswol Superwash Zermatt (wool worsted, 1¾-oz.) 17 blue (#4874, 15 gold (#4842, 8 each beige (#4825) and tan (#4843), 4 each pale lavender (#4818), lavender (#4840), grape (#4872), fuchsia (#4878, 3 wine (#4824).

Stuffing: 1 package Poly-Fil® quilt batting (stuff lightly; otherwise you'll need another package).

Hook: Size I.

Gauge: 9 sc sts = 2½ inches, 8 rounds = 3 inches.

Each stuffed pouch = 2½ by 3 inches.

Directions

1. Make 23 Stuffed Pouch Strips with 23 pouches each. Follow sample Stuffed Patch Strip procedure but work in sc (ch 10 to beg, 16 sc each rnd, 8 rnds for each pouch). Switch colors as indicated in the color chart.

2. Sew join the pattern units with yarn to match one pouch edge (push needle through inside of the pouches and pull yarn through so that you can use it to sew join again as needed).

Color Key for Color and Assembly Chart

1 = blue
2 = pale lavender
3 = lavender
4 = grape
5 = fuchsia
6 = wine
7 = gold
8 = tan
9 = beige

Graph
Pattern
Projects

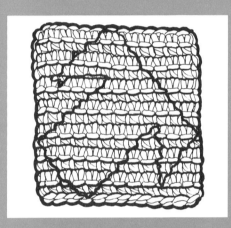

The next five projects all feature designs that are shaped with color changes. The instructions for each project are primarily visual, in the form of a graph pattern. As with other designs with color changes within a row or round, we've stuck to our rule of never carrying more than two colors at a time.

Sample Graph Patch/Octagon

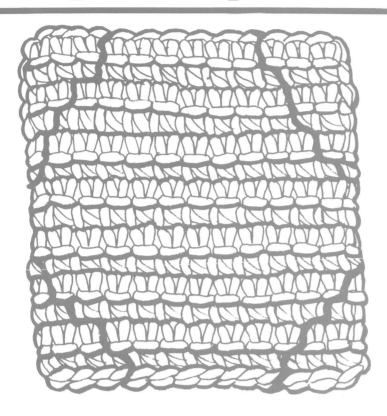

This sample patch serves as just one of the many shapes that can be worked by following a Tapestry Stitch graph instead of written instructions. Because the Octagon is such a useful patch it seemed a particularly appropriate choice to illustrate the way to plan and follow a graph as well as to compare one shape worked as shown here and from the center out as in Granny Patch Seven. Applications: Projects #31–35.

Diagram for Graphed Octagon Patch

a = color for corners b — color for center

Row 18:	aaaaaaBBBBBBaaaaaa	wrong side
Row 17:	aaaaaBBBBBBBBaaaaa	right side
Row 16:	aaaaBBBBBBBBBBaaaa	wrong side
Row 15:	aaaBBBBBBBBBBBBaaa	right side
Row 14:	aaBBBBBBBBBBBBBBaa	wrong side
Row 13:	aBBBBBBBBBBBBBBBBa	right side
Row 12:	BBBBBBBBBBBBBBBBBB	wrong side
Row 11:	BBBBBBBBBBBBBBBBBB	right side
Row 10:	BBBBBBBBBBBBBBBBBB	wrong side
Row 9:	BBBBBBBBBBBBBBBBBB	right side
Row 8:	BBBBBBBBBBBBBBBBBB	wrong side
Row 7:	BBBBBBBBBBBBBBBBBB	right side
Row 6:	aBBBBBBBBBBBBBBBBa	wrong side
Row 5:	aaBBBBBBBBBBBBBBaa	right side
Row 4:	aaaBBBBBBBBBBBBaaa	wrong side
Row 3:	aaaaBBBBBBBBBBaaaa	right side
Row 2:	aaaaaBBBBBBBBaaaaa	wrong side
Row 1:	aaaaaaBBBBBBaaaaaa	right side
Base Chain	aaaaaaBBBBBBaaaaaaA	ch 19

To Read Graphed Patterns

• All the graphed patterns in this book are for row-by-row designs. The graph therefore shows the rows worked from right to left (right side of work toward you) and also the return rows (wrong side of work toward you).

• Graphs read from the bottom up.

• The letters in the graph identify the color used, the capitalized letter at the end of the foundation chain row represents the extra chain for turning.

• The foundation chain is worked in the color that dominates the first row or in the same pattern as the first row.

#31 Tapestry T

TOP

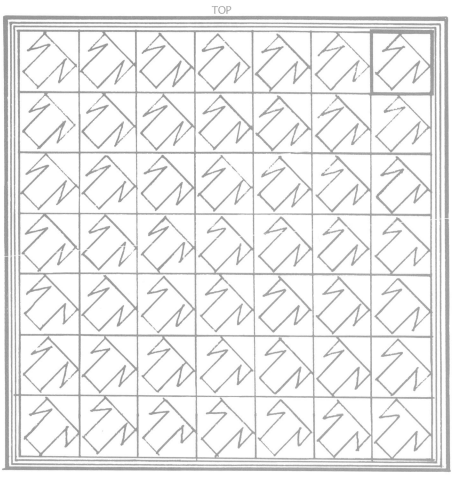

Here's another T pattern, this one worked in Tapestry Stitch. When the design strips are joined, the background metamorphoses into a second group of interlocking T units, once again illustrating our clever grandmothers' penchant for design surprises. The cloud soft yarn makes this perfect as a baby or wedding gift.
Patches Used: Graph Patch Strips.

Materials/Measurements
Finished Size: Approx. 48 by 56 inches.
Yarn: Phildar "Dedicace" (2 ply acrylic/mohair/wool 1¾-oz.) 19 Pervenche (Color A), 6 each Myosotis (Color B) and Liseron (Color C), *use each color double stranded.*
Hook: Size I.
Gauge: 7 sc sts = 2 inches, 8 rows = 2 inches.
Each T pattern = 6 × 7 inches.

Notes
• Add T units to each strip to elongate and make additional strips to widen the afghan.
• For a crisp, modern look, switch to more intense colors and a yarn that produces a non-fuzzy finish. (If you use 4-ply yarn, do not double strand.)
• For a pieced T pattern, check out project #19.

Directions

1. Sc 4 strips with 7 alternating Color B and Color C "T" motifs (beg and end with Color B). Work T pattern in these and all strips according to the graph.

2. Sc 3 strips with 7 alternating Color C and Color B "T" motifs (beg and end with Color C).

3. Join alternating strips (beg and end with a Color B "T" strip).

4. With Color B, sc into edge sts all around the joined strips (2 sc into sts before and after the corner sts—use larger hook if needed to keep border flat). End rnd with sl st in first sc. Ch 1. *Ridge st into each st around (2 sc sts in sts before and after each corner st). Ch 1. Rep from *4× (2 rnds in dark lavender and 2 in pale blue).

Diagram for Tapestry "T" Pattern

a = dark lavender B = "T" Color
After Row 23, rep rows 1–23, but switch "T" color

Row 23:	aaaaaaaaaaaaaBaaaaaaa	right side
Row 22:	aaaaaaaaaaaaaBBBBaaaaa	wrong side
Row 21:	aaaaaaaaaaaaBBBBBBaaaa	right side
Row 20:	aaaaaaaaaaBBBBBBBBaaa	wrong side
Row 19:	aaaaaaaaaBBBBBBBBBBaa	right side
Row 18:	aaaaaaaaBBBBBBBBBBBBa	wrong side
Row 17:	aaaaaaaBBBBBBBaaaaaaa	right side
Row 16:	aaaaaaBBBBBBBBBaaaaaa	wrong side
Row 15:	aaaaaBBBBBBBBBBBaaaaa	right side
Row 14:	aaaaBBBBBBBBBBBBBaaaa	wrong side
Row 13:	aaaBBBBBBBBBBBBBBBaaa	right side
Row 12:	aaBBBBBBBBBBBBBBBBaaa	wrong side
Row 11:	aBBBBBBBBBBBBBBBBBBaa	right side
Row 10:	BBBBBBBBBBBBBBBBBBBBa	wrong side
Row 9:	aBBBBBBBBBBBBBBBBBBBa	right side
Row 8:	aBBBBBBBBBBBBBBBBBBaa	wrong side
Row 7:	aaBBBBBBaBBBBBBBBBaaa	right side
Row 6:	aaaaBBBBaaBBBBBBBaaaa	wrong side
Row 5:	aaaaaBBBaaaBBBBaaaaaa	right side
Row 4:	aaaaaaBBaaaaBBBaaaaaa	wrong side
Row 3:	aaaaaaaBaaaaaBaaaaaaa	right side
Row 2:	aaaaaaaaaaaaaaaaaaaaa	wrong side
Row 1:	aaaaaaaaaaaaaaaaaaaaa	right side
Base Chain	aaaaaaaaaaaaaaaaaaaaaaA	ch 22

#32 Flower Baskets

TOP

The Flower Basket is such a popular motif that we've designed several variations. The one you see here is set straight across the square with the handle in Surface Crochet. A striped border with tiny Checkerboard Grid squares in each corner provides a handsome frame for a pretty design. Patches Used: Graph Patch.

Directions
1. Sc 20 squares with 39 sts for each of 40 rows. Follow the pattern graph for color changes.
2. With a size smaller hook, Surface Crochet the handle to the background, inserting your hook where indicated on the graph. To solidify the handle, crochet back along the Surface Crochet base, thread the yarn end into an embroidery needle and tack down against the background.
3. Add 8 rows to each edge of the square as follows:
Row 1: With baroque blue, ridge st into the sts along one edge in a gauge of 17 sts every 4 inches (adjust this gauge if your border does not lie flat). Ch 1, turn.
Row 2: Ridge st into each ridge st across. Ch 1, turn (switch to lavender).
Rows 3—8: Rep row 2 (rows 3, 4, 7 and 8 in lavender, rows 5 and 6 in baroque blue).

Materials/Measurements
Finished Size: Approx. 47 by 65 inches.
Yarn: Phildar "Lenox 084" (wool worsted, 3½-oz.) 16 lavender, 10 baroque blue.
Hook: Size I.
Gauge: 9 sts = 2 inches, 9 rows = 2 inches.
Each pattern square = 8½ inches square without border.

Notes
• To simplify and speed up the border fill-ins, crochet the little Checkerboard Grid patches two at a time.
• To see how a border like this can be worked in rounds, refer to square 13 in the Sampler (project #35).
• To see how to crochet a tilted basket, refer to project #35.
• For more of a garden feeling, use a white background.

3. Sc a Checkerboard Grid square into the spaces between the border stripes as follows: *1 sc into each of 8 edge sts (2 sc each in lavender/blue/lavender/blue). Ch 1, turn. In same colors as previous row, sc in each sc (switch to lavender on last yo). Rep from * 2× (reverse color sequence every 2 rows).

4. Sew join unattached edge of the little Checkerboard squares.

5. Join the finished Basket squares into rows (4 squares per row).

6. Join the pieced rows.

7. In colors to match edge sts, sc into each edge st around (carry and crochet around colors not in use). End rnd with sl st in first sc. Fasten off.

The Basket Pattern Graph

a = background B = basket pattern ● = handle

Row 40:	aaaaaaaaaaaaaaaaaaaaaaaaaaaaaaaaaaaaaaaa	wrong side
Row 39:	aaaaaaaaaaaaaaaaaaaaaaaaaaaaaaaaaaaaaaaa	right side
Row 38:	aaaaaaaaaaaaaaaaaaaaaaaaaaaaaaaaaaaaaaaa	wrong side
Row 37:	aaaaaaaaaaaaaaaaaaaaaaaaaaaaaaaaaaaaaaaa	right side
Row 36:	aaaaaaaaaaaaaaaaaaaaaaaaaaaaaaaaaaaaaaaa	wrong side
Row 35:	aaaaaaaaaaaaaaaaaaaaaaaaaaaaaaaaaaaaaaaa	right side
Row 34:	aaaaaaaaaaaaaaaaaaaaaaaaaaaaaaaaaaaaaaaa	wrong side
Row 33:	aaaaaaaaaaaaaaaaaaa●●●●●●aaaaaaaaaaaaaaa	right side
Row 32:	aaaaaaaaaaaaaaaa●aaaaaaa●aaaaaaaaaaaaaaa	wrong side
Row 31:	aaaaaaaaaaaaaaa●aaaaaaaaa●aaaaaaaaaaaaaa	right side
Row 30:	aaaaaaaaaaaaaa●aaaaaaaaaa●aaaaaaaaaaaaaa	wrong side
Row 29:	aaaaaaaaaaaa●aaaaaaaaaaaa●aaaaaaaaaaaaa	right side
Row 28:	aaaaaaaaaaa●aaaaaaaaaaaaa●aaaaaaaaaaaaa	wrong side
Row 27:	aaaaaaaaaa●aaaaaaaaaaaaaa●aaaaaaaaaaaaa	right side
Row 26:	aaaaaaaaa●aaaaaaaaaaaaaaa●aaaaaaaaaaaa	wrong side
Row 25:	aaaaaaaaa●aaaaaaaaaaaaaaaa●aaaaaaaaaaaa	right side
Row 24:	aaaaaaaa●aaaaaaaaaaaaaaaaa●aaaaaaaaaaaa	wrong side
Row 23:	aaaaaaa●aaaaaaaaaaaaaaaaaaa●aaaaaaaaaaa	right side
Row 22:	aaaaaa●aaaaaaaaaaaaaaaaaaaa●aaaaaaaaaaa	wrong side
Row 21:	aaaaaa●aaaaaaaaaaaaaaaaaaaaa●aaaaaaaaa	right side
Row 20:	aaaaaBBBBBBBBBBBBBBBBBBBBBBBBBBaaaaa	wrong side
Row 19:	aaaaaaBBBBBBBBBBBBBBBBBBBBBBBBBaaaaaa	right side
Row 18:	aaaaaaaBBBBBBBBBBBBBBBBBBBBBBBaaaaaaa	wrong side
Row 17:	aaaaaaaaBBBBBBBBBBBBBBBBBBBBBaaaaaaaa	right side
Row 16:	aaaaaaaaaBBBBBBBBBBBBBBBBBBBaaaaaaaaa	wrong side
Row 15:	aaaaaaaaaaBBBBBBBBBBBBBBBBBBaaaaaaaaaa	right side
Row 14:	aaaaaaaaaaaBBBBBBBBBBBBBBBBaaaaaaaaaaa	wrong side
Row 13:	aaaaaaaaaaaaBBBBBBBBBBBBBBaaaaaaaaaaaa	right side
Row 12:	aaaaaaaaaaaaaBBBBBBBBBBBBaaaaaaaaaaaaa	wrong side
Row 11:	aaaaaaaaaaaaaaBBBBBBBBBBaaaaaaaaaaaaaa	right side
Row 10:	aaaaaaaaaaaaaaBBBBBBBBBaaaaaaaaaaaaaaa	wrong side
Row 9:	aaaaaaaaaaaaaaBBBBBBBBBBaaaaaaaaaaaaaa	right side
Row 8:	aaaaaaaaaaaaaBBBBBBBBBBBBaaaaaaaaaaaaa	wrong side
Row 7:	aaaaaaaaaaaaBBBBBBBBBBBBBBaaaaaaaaaaaa	right side
Row 6:	aaaaaaaaaaaBBBBBBBBBBBBBBBBaaaaaaaaaaa	wrong side
Row 5:	aaaaaaaaaaaBBBBBBBBBBBBBBBBBBaaaaaaaaaa	right side
Row 4:	aaaaaaaaaaaaaaaaaaaaaaaaaaaaaaaaaaaaaaaa	wrong side
Row 3:	aaaaaaaaaaaaaaaaaaaaaaaaaaaaaaaaaaaaaaaa	right side
Row 2:	aaaaaaaaaaaaaaaaaaaaaaaaaaaaaaaaaaaaaaaa	wrong side
Row 1:	aaaaaaaaaaaaaaaaaaaaaaaaaaaaaaaaaaaaaaaa	right side
Base Chain	aaaaaaaaaaaaaaaaaaaaaaaaaaaaaaaaaaaaaaaaA	ch 40

#33 Hearts 'n Ruffles

TOP

What could be more appealing on a child's bed than an afghan covered with hearts? The double ruffled edge, prized for its rarity among quilters, is especially suited to the crocheter's art. The graphed pattern is sized to be used as shown, for a full-sized afghan, or for the doll size that inspired the crochet adaptation.
Patches Used: Graph Patch.

Directions
1. With white, sc 36 pattern patches in accordance with the pattern graph (18 with blue and 18 with pink Hearts).
2. With blue, *sc into the edge sts all around each patch with a pink Heart (3 sc into the corner sts). End rnd with sl st join to the first sc. Ch 1. Rep from *2×, once with blue and once with white.
3. With pink, sc around each patch with a blue Heart, following step 2 procedure.
4. Join the finished patches into rows (6 per row).
5. Join the rows.

Materials/Measurements
Finished Size: Approx. 45 by 48 inches.
Yarn: Plymouth "Saxony II" (2 ply wool worsted, 3½-oz.) 7 natural, 2 each pink heather and powder blue.
Hook: Size I.
Gauge: 7 sts = 2 inches, 4 rows = 1 inch
Each Heart unit = 6 × 5½ inches without border,

Notes
• If you switch to more sharply contrasted colors, refer to the Stretch-in-Back technique Tapestry Stitch in *GENERAL INSTRUCTIONS*.
• For a rectangular afghan, make 10 rows with 6 patches each. For a doll-sized afghan, make 12 patches for 4 rows of 3 patches each.
• If you want to make another double ruffled afghan with a different design patch, substitute 4 Double Triangles for the Hearts (each the same size as the Double Triangle sample patch).

To Make Double Scallop Border

Round 1: (Shell 1) With white (right side toward you now and throughout, beg at any corner, hook into the front half of st loop), 1 sc into each of the first 2 sts, *2 dc in each of the next 2 sts, 3 tr in next st, 1 dc in each of next 2 sts, 1 sc in each of the next 5 sts. Rep from * all around (1 sc in each of the 2 sts before the corner, 3 sc in each corner st, 1 sc in each of the next 2 sts). End rnd with sl st join to the first sc (sl st through in pink or blue). Ch 1.
A Word to the Wise. As you near the corners, you may have to adjust some of the stitches in order to fit the small shell into the corner.
Round 2: (Shell 1) With pink or blue, crochet into front loop of each st (sc into each sc, dc in each dc, tr in each tr). Fasten off.
Round 1: (Shell 2) With white, work second rnd of shells in back of first. To do so, insert hook into the other half (the back loops) of the edge sts into which you worked the first row of the first shell. In order for these shells to fall between the others, work 1 sc into each of the first 6 sts after the corner before you rep shell pattern.
Round 2: (Shell 2) With pink or blue (blue, if first shell was pink), rep rnd 2 of first shell. Fasten off.

Hearts 'n Ruffles Pattern Graph

a = background   B = heart pattern

Row 24:	aaaaaaaaaaaaaaaaaaaaaa	wrong side
Row 23:	aaaaaaaaaaaaaaaaaaaaaa	right side
Row 22:	aaaaaaaaaaaaaaaaaaaaaa	wrong side
Row 21:	aaaaaaaaaaaaaaaaaaaaaa	right side
Row 20:	aaaaaaaaaaaaaaaaaaaaaa	wrong side
Row 19:	aaaaaaaaaaaaaaaaaaaaaa	right side
Row 18:	aaaaaaaaaaaaaaaaaaaaaa	wrong side
Row 17:	aaaaaaaBaaaaaBaaaaaaa	right side
Row 16:	aaaaaaBBBaaaBBBaaaaaa	wrong side
Row 15:	aaaaaBBBBBaBBBBBaaaaa	right side
Row 14:	aaaaBBBBBBBBBBBBaaaa	wrong side
Row 13:	aaaaBBBBBBBBBBBBBaaaa	right side
Row 12:	aaaaBBBBBBBBBBBBBaaaa	wrong side
Row 11:	aaaaBBBBBBBBBBBBBaaaa	right side
Row 10:	aaaaaBBBBBBBBBBBaaaaa	wrong side
Row 9:	aaaaaaBBBBBBBBBaaaaaa	right side
Row 8:	aaaaaaaBBBBBBBaaaaaaa	wrong side
Row 7:	aaaaaaaaBBBBBaaaaaaaa	right side
Row 6:	aaaaaaaaaBBBaaaaaaaaa	wrong side
Row 5:	aaaaaaaaaaBaaaaaaaaaa	right side
Row 4:	aaaaaaaaaaaaaaaaaaaaaa	wrong side
Row 3:	aaaaaaaaaaaaaaaaaaaaaa	right side
Row 2:	aaaaaaaaaaaaaaaaaaaaaa	wrong side
Row 1:	aaaaaaaaaaaaaaaaaaaaaa	right side
Base Chain	aaaaaaaaaaaaaaaaaaaaaaA	ch 22

#34 House on the Hill

TOP

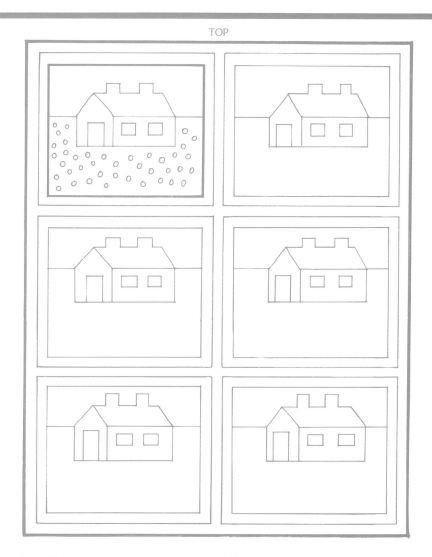

The most representational of all the old-time designs are those generally classified as House patterns. Whether it's a schoolhouse, cottage, barn or church, the House is always capped with a chimney. The most unusual examples feature details from the surrounding landscape, as does our House on the Hill with its picot flower garden.

Directions

The House on the Hill Patch Make 6: 1 each in the following color combinations for house, roof and door: white/rust/pink, white/brown/rust, pink/plum/white, yellow/rust/white, brown/yellow/white, rust/plum/yellow. Grass and sky sections are the same throughout.
With green, ch 51.
Row 1: Sc in each ch (50 sets). Ch 1, turn now and throughout.
Rows 2–4: Sc in each sc.
Rows 5–22: Cont to sc across, but intersperse picots on all rows with right side toward you as indicated in chart (letter p). Use the same color for all picots in each of 9 rows (the color sequence for rows 5, 7, 9, 11, 13, 15, 17, 19 and 21 is yellow/white/pink/plum/rust/white/yellow/pink/rust). To make the picots, attach a 3-yard length of the picot color at the beg of the row. Work as detailed in *GENERAL INSTRUCTIONS—Bump Stitches*, following the graph for spacing the picots across the row.

Materials/Measurements
Finished Size: Approx. 36 by 56 inches.
Yarn: Unger "Aries" (4 ply acrylic and wool orlon, 3½-oz.) 3 each green (#435) and blue (#419), 2 each pink (#405) and plum (#403), 1 each white (#580), yellow (#435), rust (#440) and brown (#451).
Hook: Size J.
Gauge: 3 sts = 1 inch, 3 rows = 1 inch.
Each house patch = 16 inches square without border.

Notes
• If you want an afghan with more and smaller patches, use yarn and hook to give you a 4 stitch per inch gauge.
• Many quilt patterns use the same colors for every house. To apply this format to the illustrated afghan, crochet the houses in a bright blue or red, with white doors and windows and a lemon gold sky.
• Folded down the center and then into squares, your afghan can do double duty as a generously proportioned sofa pillow.

Rows 23–36: Work in 3 separate sections as follows:
Section 1: Work as in rows 5–23 for 8 sts (the right edge). Work just one or two picots into each picot row, selecting picot colors at random. Fasten off.
Section 2: Rep Section 1, at the left edge.
Section 3: Follow the chart to ridge st into each of 34 sc in the middle of row 23, then cont in sc. Sew join the open edges between the grass and house sections.

Rows 37–42: Work in 2 sections as follows:
Section 1: (Wrong side toward you) with colors indicated in graph pattern, 1 sc in each of 22 sc (the last row of grass section at left edge). Ch 1, turn and cont through row 42 (make a dec in the first 2 sc on rows 38, 40 and 42 and in the last 2 sc on rows 39 and 41.
Section 2: Go back to row 37. With colors indicated in graph (right side toward you), sc into each of 9 sc (the right grass edge), ridge st in the next 19 sc (part of the house). In the roof color, sl st to the row 37 edge of section 1, sl st into the edge st immediately above it. Ch 1, turn. Cont to ridge st in roof color sts and sc in grass color sts as indicated in graph pattern (through row 42).
A Word to the Wise. When you slip stitch the ridge stitched roof section to the triangular roof section, you increase the ridge stitched roof edge and crochet join the edges of the first and second sections.

Rows 43–54: 50 sts across each row according to graph pattern, sc in each sc, ridge st into ridge sts (the rest of the roof and the 2 chimneys).

To Finish, Join and Make Border

1. Using roof color, Surface crochet up and down the peak and roof corner of house, as shown in graph.
2. With pink sc into the edge sts around each pattern square (dec gauge to 11 sts every 4 inches—adjust if there's any rippling or pulling). End rnd with sl st join to first sc. Ch 1, turn.
3. *Ridge st into each sc around (2 sc into sts before and after each corner st). Sl st in first ridge st (sl st through in plum). rep from *1 ×. Fasten off.
4. Join house patches into one strip with a white, pink and yellow house (top to bottom) and a second strip with a rust, yellow and white house (top to bottom).
5. Join the strips down the center.
6. With right side toward you, ridge st into edge sts all around in same gauge used in step 2. End rnd with sl st join. Ch 1 turn. Ridge st into each ridge st (2 sc in sts before and after each corner st), sl st in first ridge st. Fasten off.

House on the Hill Graph

Color and Stitch Key

g = green   P = picot   h = house color   D = door color
X = door knob color   b = blue   r = roof color/ridge st
right/wrong = rows are worked in segments with different sides toward you

Row 54:	bbbbbbbbbbbbbbbbbbbbbbbbbbbbbbbbbbbbbbbbbbbbbbbb	wrong side
Row 53:	bbbbbbbbbbbbbbbbbbbbbbbbbbbbbbbbbbbbbbbbbbbbbbbb	right side
Row 52:	bbbbbbbbbbbbbbbbbbbbbbbbbbbbbbbbbbbbbbbbbbbbbbbb	wrong side
Row 51:	bbbbbbbbbbbbbbbbbbbbbbbbbbbbbbbbbbbbbbbbbbbbbbbb	right side
Row 50:	bbbbbbbbbbbbbbbbbbbbbbbbbbbbbbbbbbbbbbbbbbbbbbbb	wrong side
Row 49:	bbbbbbbbbbbbbbbbbbbbbbbbbbbbbbbbbbbbbbbbbbbbbbbb	right side
Row 48:	bbbbbbbbbbbbbnnnrrrbbbbbbbbbbbbrrrbbbbbbbbbbbbbbbbbb	wrong side
Row 47:	bbbbbbbbbbbbbbbrrrbbbbbbbbbbbbrrrbbbbbbbbbbbbbbbbbb	right side
Row 46:	bbbbbbbbbbbbbbbrrrrbbbbbbbbbbbrrrbbbbbbbbbbbbbbbbbb	wrong side
Row 45:	bbbbbbbbbbbbbbbrrrbbbbbbbbbbbbrrrbbbbbbbbbbbbbbbbbb	right side
Row 44:	bbbbbbbbbbbbbbbrrrrrrrrrrrrrrrrrbbbbbbbbbbbbbbbbbb	wrong side
Row 43:	bbbbbbbbbbbbbbbrrrrrrrrrrrrrrrrrrbbbbbbbbbbbbbbbb	right side
Row 42:	bbbbbbbbbbbbbbbbhrrrrrrrrrrrrrrrrrrrbbbbbbbbbbbbbb	right/wrong
Row 41:	bbbbbbbbbbbbbbbhhhrrrrrrrrrrrrrrrrrrrbbbbbbbbbbbbb	right/wrong
Row 40:	bbbbbbbbbbbbbhhhhhrrrrrrrrrrrrrrrrrrrrbbbbbbbbbbbb	right/wrong
Row 39:	bbbbbbbbbbbbhhhhhhhrrrrrrrrrrrrrrrrrrrrrbbbbbbbbbbb	right/wrong
Row 38:	bbbbbbbbbbbhhhhhhhhhrrrrrrrrrrrrrrrrrrrrrrbbbbbbbbb	right/wrong
Row 37:	bbbbbbbbbbhhhhhhhhhhhrrrrrrrrrrrrrrrrrrrrrrrbbbbbbbb	right/wrong
Row 36:	gggggggghhhhhhhhhhhhhhhhhhhhhhhhhhhhhhhggggggggg	wrong side
Row 35:	ggPggPgghhhhhhhhhhhhhhhhhhhhhhhhhhhhhhhggPggPgg	right side
Row 34:	gggggggghhhhhhhhhhhhhhhhhhhhhhhhhhhhhhhggggggggg	wrong side
Row 33:	gPggPggghhhhhhhhhhhhhhhhhhhhhhhhhhhhhhhhhggPggPgg	right side
Row 32:	gggggggghhhhhhhhhhhhhhhhhhhhhhhhhhhhhhhggggggggg	wrong side
Row 31:	gPggPggghhhhhhhhhhhhhhhhhhhhhhhhhhhhhhhhhggPggggg	right side
Row 30:	gggggggghhhhhDDDDDhhhhhhhhDDhhhhhDDDhhhhggggggggg	wrong side
Row 29:	ggPgPggghhhhhDDDDDDhhhhhhhhDDDhhhhhDDDhhhhggPggPgg	right side
Row 28:	gggggggghhhhhDDDDDhhhhhhhhhDDDhhhhhDDDhhhhggggggggg	wrong side
Row 27:	ggPgggggghhhhhDDDDXDhhhhhhhhDDDhhhhhDDDhhhhgggPggggg	right side
Row 26:	gggggggghhhhhDDDDXDhhhhhhhhhhhhhhhhhhhhhhhggggggggg	wrong side
Row 25:	ggPggPgghhhhhDDDDDhhhhhhhhhhhhhhhhhhhhhhhgPggPggg	right side
Row 24:	gggggggghhhhhDDDDDhhhhhhhhhhhhhhhhhhhhhhhggggggggg	wrong side
Row 23:	ggggPggghhhhhDDDDDDhhhhhhhhhhhhhhhhhhhhhhhhgPgggPgg	right side
Row 22:	gggggggggggggggggggggggggggggggggggggggggggggggg	wrong side
Row 21:	gggggggPgggggPgggggPgggggPgggggPgggggPgggggPggggg	right side
Row 20:	gggggggggggggggggggggggggggggggggggggggggggggggg	wrong side
Row 19:	ggggPgggggPgggggPgggggPgggggPgggggPgggggPgggggPggg	right side
Row 18:	gggggggggggggggggggggggggggggggggggggggggggggggg	wrong side
Row 17:	gggggggPgggggPgggggPgggggPgggggPgggggPgggggPggggg	right side
Row 16:	gggggggggggggggggggggggggggggggggggggggggggggggg	wrong side
Row 15:	ggggPgggggPgggggPgggggPgggggPgggggPgggggPgggggPggg	right side
Row 14:	gggggggggggggggggcggggggggggggggggggggggggggggggg	wrong side
Row 13:	gggggggPgggggPgggggPgggggPgggggPgggggPgggggPggggg	right side
Row 12:	gggggggggggggggggggggggggggggggggggggggggggggggg	wrong side
Row 11:	ggggPgggggPgggggPgggggPgggggPgggggPgggggPgggggPggg	right side
Row 10:	gggggggggggggggggggggggggggggggggggggggggggggggg	wrong side
Row 9:	gggggggPgggggPgggggPgggggPgggggPgggggPgggggPggggg	right side
Row 8:	gggggggggggggggggggggggggggggggggggggggggggggggg	wrong side
Row 7:	ggggPgggggPgggggPgggggPgggggPgggggPgggggPgggggPggg	right side
Row 6:	gggggggggggggggggggggggggggggggggggggggggggggggg	wrong side
Row 5:	gggggggPgggggPgggggPgggggPgggggPgggggPgggggPggggg	right side
Row 4:	gggggggggggggggggggggggggggggggggggggggggggggggg	wrong side
Row 3:	gggggggggggggggggggggggggggggggggggggggggggggggg	right side
Row 2:	gggggggggggggggggggggggggggggggggggggggggggggggg	wrong side
Row 1:	gggggggggggggggggggggggggggggggggggggggggggggggg	right side
Base Chain	gggggggggggggggggggggggggggggggggggggggggggggggggG	ch 51

153

#35 Sampler

TOP

By now you're familiar with some of the more popular quilt patterns and the techniques for re-creating them with crochet hook and yarn. For our finale, here's a medley of patterns to assemble into a sampler afghan or a rug. Each square is a stepping stone to another project.

Materials/Measurements
Finished Size: Approx. 41 by 67 inches.
Yarn: Unger "Aries" (4-ply wool and acrylic, 3½ oz); 4 brown (#451), 3 each beige (#454), and rust (#430).
Hook: Size I.
Gauge: 13 sts = 4 inches, 13 rows = 4 inches.
Each patch = Approx 11 inches square without border, 13 inches square bordered.

Notes
• All squares are worked in single crochet with ridge stitched borders.
• Some squares will be slightly smaller than the rest. You can compensate for this by single crocheting once around in colors to match the edge stitches.
• If you use squares 7–12 for another afghan, you can enlarge the individual components and piece as four separate patches.

Square One/Tilted Basket

A tilted variation of the basket in project #32. The graph pattern illustrates the row-by-row procedure, as well as where to insert your hook for the Surface Crochet handle.

Color Key a = beige B = brown
Outlined letters indicate where to insert hook for Surface Crochet handle

Row 36:	aaaaaaaaaaaaaaaaaaaaaaaaaaaaaaaaaaaa	wrong side
Row 35:	aaaaaaaaaaaaaaaaaaaaaaaaaaaaaaaaaaaa	right side
Row 34:	aaaaaaaaaaaaaaaaaaaaaaaaaaaaBaaaaaaa	wrong side
Row 33:	aaaaaaaaaaaaaaaaaaaaaaaaaaaBBaaaaaaa	wrong side
Row 32:	aaaaaaaaaaaⓐaaⓐaaⓐaaⓐaaaBBBaaaaaaa	wrong side
Row 31:	aaaaaaaaaⓐaaaaaaaaaaaaaaBBBBaaaaaaa	right side
Row 30:	aaaaaaaⓐaaaaaaaaaaaaaaaaBBBBBaaaaaaa	wrong side
Row 29:	aaaaaaaaaaaaaaaaaaaaaaaaBBBBBBaaaaaaa	right side
Row 28:	aaaaⓐaaaaaaaaaaaaaaaaaaaBBBBBBaaaaaaa	wrong side
Row 27:	aaaaaaaaaaaaaaaaaaaaaaaaBBBBBBBaaaaaaa	right side
Row 26:	aaⓐaaaaaaaaaaaaaaaaaaaaBBBBBBBBaaaaaaa	wrong side
Row 25:	aaaaaaaaaaaaaaaaaaaaaaBBBBBBBBBaaaaaaa	right side
Row 24:	aaⓐaaaaaaaaaaaaaaaaaaaBBBBBBBBBaaaaaaa	wrong side
Row 23:	aaaaaaaaaaaaaaaaaaaaaBBBBBBBBBBBaaaaaaa	right side
Row 22:	aⓐaaaaaaaaaaaaaaaBBBBBBBBBBBBaaaaaaa	wrong side
Row 21:	aaaaaaaaaaaaaaaBBBBBBBBBBBBBaaaaaaa	right side
Row 20:	aⓐaaaaaaaaaaaaBBBBBBBBBBBBBBaaaaaaa	wrong side
Row 19:	aaaaaaaaaaaaaBBBBBBBBBBBBBBBaaaaaaa	right side
Row 18:	aaⓐaaaaaaaaaBBBBBBBBBBBBBBBBaaaaaaa	wrong side
Row 17:	aaaaaaaaaaaBBBBBBBBBBBBBBBBBaaaaaaa	right side
Row 16:	aaⓐaaaaaaaBBBBBBBBBBBBBBBBBBaaaaaaa	wrong side
Row 15:	aaaaaaaaaBBBBBBBBBBBBBBBBBBBaaaaaaa	right side
Row 14:	aaⓐaaaaaBBBBBBBBBBBBBBBBBBBBaaaaaaa	wrong side
Row 13:	aaaaaaaBBBBBBBBBBBBBBBBBBBBBBaaaaaaa	right side
Row 12:	aaaⓐaBBBBBBBBBBBBBBBBBBBBBBBBBBBB	wrong side
Row 11:	aaaaBBBBBBBBBBBBBBBBBBBBBBBBBBBBBa	right side
Row 10:	aaaBBBBBBBBBBBBBBBBBBBBBBBBBBBBBaa	wrong side
Row 9:	aaBBBBBBBBBBBBBBBBBBBBBBBBBBBBBaaa	right side
Row 8:	aBBBBBBBBBBBBBBBBBBBBBBBBBBBBBaaaa	wrong side
Row 7:	BBBBBBBBBBBBBBBBBBBBBBBBBBBBBaaaaa	right side
Row 6:	aaaaaaaaaaaaaaaaaaaaaaaaBBBBBaaaaaa	wrong side
Row 5:	aaaaaaaaaaaaaaaaaaaaaaaaaBBBBaaaaaaa	right side
Row 4:	aaaaaaaaaaaaaaaaaaaaaaaaaaBBBBaaaaaaa	wrong side
Row 3:	aaaaaaaaaaaaaaaaaaaaaaaaaaBBBaaaaaaaa	right side
Row 2:	aaaaaaaaaaaaaaaaaaaaaaaaaaBBaaaaaaaaaa	wrong side
Row 1:	aaaaaaaaaaaaaaaaaaaaaaaaaaBaaaaaaaaaaa	right side
Base Chain	aaaaaaaaaaaaaaaaaaaaaaaaaaaaaaaaaaaaaA	ch 37

Square Two/Sailboat

This sea-worthy little boat is a relative latecomer to the quilt scene having made its debut during the 1930s. It's been sailing on a wave of popularity ever since. See pattern graph for detailed instructions.

a = beige B = brown c = rust

Row 36:	aaaaaaaaaaaaaaaaaaaaaaaaaaaaaaaaaaaa	wrong
Row 35:	aaaaaaaaaaaaaaaaaaaaaaaaaaaaaaaaaaaa	right
Row 34:	aaaaaaaaaacaaaaaaacaaaaaaaaaaaaaaaaa	wrong
Row 33:	aaaaaaaaaaccaaaaaaccaaaaaaaaaaaaaaaa	right
Row 32:	aaaaaaaaaacccaaaaacccaaaaaaaaaaaaaaa	wrong
Row 31:	aaaaaaaaaaccccaaaaccccaaaaaaaaaaaaaa	right
Row 30:	aaaaaaaaaacccccaaacccccaaaaaaaaaaaaa	wrong
Row 29:	aaaaaaaaaaccccccaaccccccaaaaaaaaaaaa	right
Row 28:	aaaaaaaaaacccccccaccccccccaaaaaaaaaa	wrong
Row 27:	aaaaaaaaaaccccccccccccccccaaaaaaaaaa	right
Row 26:	aaaaaaaaaacaaaaaaacaaaaaaaaaaaaaaaaa	wrong
Row 25:	aaaaaaaaaaccaaaaaaccaaaaaaaaaaaaaaaa	right
Row 24:	aaaaaaaaaacccaaaaacccaaaaaaaaaaaaaaa	wrong
Row 23:	aaaaaaaaaaccccaaaaccccaaaaaaaaaaaaaa	right
Row 22:	aaaaaaaaaacccccaaacccccaaaaaaaaaaaaa	wrong
Row 21:	aaaaaaaaaaccccccaaccccccaaaaaaaaaaaa	right
Row 20:	aaaaaaaaaacccccccaccccccaaaaaaaaaaaa	wrong
Row 19:	aaaaaaaaaaccccccccccccccccaaaaaaaaaa	right
Row 18:	aaaBBBBBBBBBBBBBBBBBBBBBBBBBBaaa	wrong
Row 17:	aaaaBBBBBBBBBBBBBBBBBBBBBBBBBaaaa	right
Row 16:	aaaaaBBBBBBBBBBBBBBBBBBBBBBBBaaaaa	wrong
Row 15:	aaaaaaBBBBBBBBBBBBBBBBBBBBBBBaaaaaa	right
Row 14:	aaaaaaaBBBBBBBBBBBBBBBBBBBBBaaaaaaa	wrong
Row 13:	aaaaaaaaBBBBBBBBBBBBBBBBBBBBaaaaaaaa	right
Row 12:	aaaaaaaaaBBBBBBBBBBBBBBBBBBaaaaaaaaa	wrong
Row 11:	aaaaaaaaaaBBBBBBBBBBBBBBBBaaaaaaaaaa	right
Row 10:	aaaaaaaaaaaaaaaaaaaaaaaaaaaaaaaaaaaa	wrong
Row 9:	aaaaaaaaaaaaaaaaaaaaaaaaaaaaaaaaaaaa	right
Row 8:	aaaaaaaaaaaaaaaaaaaaaaaaaaaaaaaaaaaa	wrong
Row 7:	aaaaaaaaaaaaaaaaaaaaaaaaaaaaaaaaaaaa	right
Row 6:	aaaaaaaaaaaaaaaaaaaaaaaaaaaaaaaaaaaa	wrong
Row 5:	aaaaaaaaaaaaaaaaaaaaaaaaaaaaaaaaaaaa	right
Row 4:	aaaaaaaaaaaaaaaaaaaaaaaaaaaaaaaaaaaa	wrong
Row 3:	aaaaaaaaaaaaaaaaaaaaaaaaaaaaaaaaaaaa	right
Row 2:	aaaaaaaaaaaaaaaaaaaaaaaaaaaaaaaaaaaa	wrong
Row 1:	aaaaaaaaaaaaaaaaaaaaaaaaaaaaaaaaaaaa	right
Base Chain	aaaaaaaaaaaaaaaaaaaaaaaaaaaaaaaaaaaaA	ch 37

Square Three/Double Triangle Square Basket

Another tilted basket. This one offers a good opportunity to practice crocheting several double triangles in a row. The graph pattern again shows where to add the Surface Crochet handle.

a = beige B = rust ● = surface crochet

Row 36:	aaaaaaaaaaaaaaaaaaaaaaaaaaaaaBaaaaaa	wrong
Row 35:	aaaaaaaaaaaaaaaaaaaaaaaaaaaaBBaaaaaa	right
Row 34:	aaaaaaaaaaaaaaaaaaaaaaaaaaaaBBBaaaaaa	wrong
Row 33:	aaaaaaaaaaaaaaaaaaaaaaaaaaaBBBBaaaaaa	right
Row 32:	aaaaaaaaaaaaaaaaaaaaaaaaaaaBBBBBaaaaaa	wrong
Row 31:	aaaaaaaaaaaaaaaaaaaaaaaaaaaBBBBBBaaaaaa	right

end 4th set 2 triangle squares

Row 30:	aaaaaaaaaaaaaaaaaaaaaaaaaBaaaaaBaaaaaa	wrong
Row 29:	aaaaaaaaaaaaaaaaaaaaaaaaaBBaaaaBBaaaaaa	right
Row 28:	aaaaaaaaaaaaaaaaaaaaaaaaaBBBaaaBBBaaaaaa	wrong
Row 27:	aaaaaaaaaaaaaaaaaaaaaaaaBBBBaaBBBBaaaaaa	right
Row 26:	aaaaaaaaaaaaaaaaaaaaaaaaBBBBBaBBBBBaaaaaa	wrong
Row 25:	aaaaaaaaaaaaaaaaaaaaaaaaBBBBBBBBBBBaaaaaa	right

end 3rd set 3 triangle squares

Row 24:	aaaaaaaaaaaaaaaaaBaaaaaBaaaaaBaaaaaa	wrong
Row 23:	aaaaaaaaaaaaaaaaaBBaaaaBBaaaaBBaaaaaa	right
Row 22:	aaaaaaaaaaaaaaaaaBBBaaaBBBaaaBBBaaaaaa	wrong
Row 21:	aaaaaaaaaaaaaaaaBBBBaaBBBBaaBBBBaaaaaa	right
Row 20:	aaaaaaaaaaaaaaaaBBBBBaBBBBBaBBBBBaaaaaa	wrong
Row 19:	aaaaaaaaaaaaaaaaBBBBBBBBBBBBBBBBaaaaaa	right

end 2nd set 4 triangle squares

Row 18:	aaaaaaaaaaaaBaaaaaBaaaaaBaaaaaBaaaaaa	wrong
Row 17:	aaaaaaaaaaaaBBaaaaBBaaaaBBaaaaBBaaaaaa	right
Row 16:	aaaaaaaaaaaBBBaaaBBBaaaBBBaaaBBBaaaaaa	wrong
Row 15:	aaaaaaaaaaBBBBaaBBBBaaBBBBaaBBBBaaaaaa	right
Row 14:	aaaaaaaaaBBBBBaBBBBBaBBBBBaBBBBBaaaaaa	wrong
Row 13:	aaaaaaBBBBBBBBBBBBBBBBBBBBBBBBaaaaaa	right

end first 4 triangle squares

Row 12:	aaaaaBaaaaaBaaaaaBaaaaaBaaaaaaBBBBBB	wrong
Row 11:	aaaaBBaaaaBBaaaaBBaaaaBBaaaaaaBBBBBa	right
Row 10:	aaaBBBaaaBBBaaaBBBaaaBBBaaaaaaBBBBaa	wrong
Row 9:	aaBBBBaaBBBBaaBBBBaaaaaaBBBaaa	right
Row 8:	aBBBBBaBBBBBaBBBBBaaaaaaBBaaaa	wrong
Row 7:	BBBBBBBBBBBBBBBBBBBBBaaaaaaBaaaaa	right
Row 6:	aaaaaaaaaaaaaaaaaaaaaaaaaBBBBBBaaaaaa	wrong
Row 5:	aaaaaaaaaaaaaaaaaaaaaaaaaBBBBBaaaaaaa	right
Row 4:	aaaaaaaaaaaaaaaaaaaaaaaaaaBBBBaaaaaaaa	wrong
Row 3:	aaaaaaaaaaaaaaaaaaaaaaaaaaaBBBaaaaaaaaa	right
Row 2:	aaaaaaaaaaaaaaaaaaaaaaaaaaaBBaaaaaaaaaa	wrong
Row 1:	aaaaaaaaaaaaaaaaaaaaaaaaaaaBaaaaaaaaaaa	right
Base Chain	aaaaaaaaaaaaaaaaaaaaaaaaaaaaaaaaaaaaA	ch 37

Square Four/ Row-by-Row Snail's Trail

A less op-arty, row-by-row made variation of Snail's Trail (project #24). See pattern graph for detailed instructions. If you need a final round of edging to align this square to some of the others, be sure to switch colors to match the edge pattern.

a = beige B = brown

Row 34:	BBBBaaaaBBBBBBaaaaaaBBBBBBaaaaBBBB	wrong
Row 33:	aaaaBBBBaaaaaaBBBBBBaaaaaaBBBBaaaa	right
Row 32:	aaaaBBBBaaaaaaBBBBBBaaaaaaBBBBaaaa	wrong
Row 31:	aaaaBBBBaaaaaaBBBBBBaaaaaaBBBBaaaa	right
Row 30:	BBBBaaaaBBBBBBaaaaaaBBBBBBaaaaBBBB	wrong
Row 29:	BBBBaaaaBBBBBBaaaaaaBBBBBBaaaaBBBB	right
Row 28:	BBBBaaaaBBBBBBaaaaaaBBBBBBaaaaBBBB	wrong
Row 27:	BBBBaaaaBBBBBBaaaaaaBBBBBBaaaaBBBB	right
Row 26:	aaaaBBBBaaaaaaBBBBBBaaaaaaBBBBaaaa	wrong
Row 25:	aaaaBBBBaaaaaaBBBBBBaaaaaaBBBBaaaa	right
Row 24:	aaaaBBBBaaaaaaBBBBBBaaaaaaBBBBaaaa	wrong
Row 23:	aaaaBBBBaaaaaaBBBBBBaaaaaaBBBBaaaa	right
Row 22:	aaaaBBBBaaaaaaBBBBBBaaaaaaBBBBaaaa	wrong
Row 21:	aaaaBBBBaaaaaaBBBBBBaaaaaaBBBBaaaa	right
Row 20:	BBBBaaaaBBBBBBaaaaaaBBBBBBaaaaBBBB	wrong
Row 19:	BBBBaaaaBBBBBBaaaaaaBBBBBBaaaaBBBB	right
Row 18:	BBBBaaaaBBBBBBaaaaaaBBBBBBaaaaBBBB	wrong
Row 17:	BBBBaaaaBBBBBBaaaaaaBBBBBBaaaaBBBB	right
Row 16:	BBBBaaaaBBBBBBaaaaaaBBBBBBaaaaBBBB	wrong
Row 15:	BBBBaaaaBBBBBBaaaaaaBBBBBBaaaaBBBB	right
Row 14:	aaaaBBBBaaaaaaBBBBBBaaaaaaBBBBaaaa	wrong
Row 13:	aaaaBBBBaaaaaaBBBBBBaaaaaaBBBBaaaa	right
Row 12:	aaaaBBBBaaaaaaBBBBBBaaaaaaBBBBaaaa	wrong
Row 11:	aaaaBBBBaaaaaaBBBBBBaaaaaaBBBBaaaa	right
Row 10:	aaaaBBBBaaaaaaBBBBBBaaaaaaBBBBaaaa	wrong
Row 9:	aaaaBBBBaaaaaaBBBBBBaaaaaaBBBBaaaa	right
Row 8:	BBBBaaaaBBBBBBaaaaaaBBBBBBaaaaBBBB	wrong
Row 7:	BBBBaaaaBBBBBBaaaaaaBBBBBBaaaaBBBB	right
Row 6:	BBBBaaaaBBBBBBaaaaaaBBBBBBaaaaBBBB	wrong
Row 5:	BBBBaaaaBBBBBBaaaaaaBBBBBBaaaaBBBB	right
Row 4:	aaaaBBBBaaaaaaBBBBBBaaaaaaBBBBaaaa	wrong
Row 3:	aaaaBBBBaaaaaaBBBBBBaaaaaaBBBBaaaa	right
Row 2:	aaaaBBBBaaaaaaBBBBBBaaaaaaBBBBaaaa	wrong
Row 1:	BBBBaaaaBBBBBBaaaaaaBBBBBBaaaaBBBB	right
Base Chain	BBBBaaaaBBBBBBaaaaaaBBBBBBaaaaBBBBB	ch 35

Square Five/Road

A simple road pattern. As you follow the graph pattern, you'll see that the "road" is paved diagonally across a square made with Plain Patches and Double Triangle Squares, worked 4 patches across the row.

a = beige B = brown

Row 36:	aaaaaaaaaaBaaaaaaaaaaaaaaaaaaaBBBBBBBBB	wrong side
Row 35:	aaaaaaaaaaBBaaaaaaaaaaaaaaaaaaBBBBBBBB	right side
Row 34:	aaaaaaaaaaBBBaaaaaaaaaaaaaaaaaaBBBBBBB	wrong side
Row 33:	aaaaaaaaaaBBBBaaaaaaaaaaaaaaaaaaBBBBBB	right side
Row 32:	aaaaaaaaaaBBBBBaaaaaaaaaaaaaaaaaaBBBBB	wrong side
Row 31:	aaaaaaaaaaBBBBBBaaaaaaaaaaaaaaaaaaBBBB	right side
Row 30:	aaaaaaaaaaBBBBBBBaaaaaaaaaaaaaaaaaaBBB	wrong side
Row 29:	aaaaaaaaaaBBBBBBBBaaaaaaaaaaaaaaaaaaBB	right side
Row 28:	aaaaaaaaaaBBBBBBBBBaaaaaaaaaaaaaaaaaaB	wrong side
Row 27:	BBBBBBBBaaaaaaaaaBaaaaaaaaaaaaaaaaaa	right side
Row 26:	aBBBBBBBBaaaaaaaaaBBaaaaaaaaaaaaaaaaa	wrong side
Row 25:	aaBBBBBBBaaaaaaaaaBBBaaaaaaaaaaaaaaaa	right side
Row 24:	aaaBBBBBBaaaaaaaaaBBBBaaaaaaaaaaaaaaa	wrong side
Row 23:	aaaaBBBBBaaaaaaaaaBBBBBaaaaaaaaaaaaaa	right side
Row 22:	aaaaaBBBBaaaaaaaaaBBBBBBaaaaaaaaaaaaa	wrong side
Row 21:	aaaaaaBBBaaaaaaaaaBBBBBBBaaaaaaaaaaaa	right side
Row 20:	aaaaaaaBBaaaaaaaaaBBBBBBBBaaaaaaaaaaa	wrong side
Row 19:	aaaaaaaaBaaaaaaaaaBBBBBBBBBaaaaaaaaaa	right side
Row 18:	aaaaaaaaaBBBBBBBBBaaaaaaaaaBaaaaaaaaa	wrong side
Row 17:	aaaaaaaaaaBBBBBBBBaaaaaaaaaBBaaaaaaaa	right side
Row 16:	aaaaaaaaaaaBBBBBBBaaaaaaaaaBBBaaaaaaa	wrong side
Row 15:	aaaaaaaaaaaaBBBBBBaaaaaaaaaBBBBaaaaaa	right side
Row 14:	aaaaaaaaaaaaaBBBBBaaaaaaaaaBBBBBaaaaa	wrong side
Row 13:	aaaaaaaaaaaaaaBBBBaaaaaaaaaBBBBBBaaa	right side
Row 12:	aaaaaaaaaaaaaaaBBBaaaaaaaaaBBBBBBBaa	wrong side
Row 11:	aaaaaaaaaaaaaaaaBBaaaaaaaaaBBBBBBBB	right side
Row 10:	aaaaaaaaaaaaaaaaaBaaaaaaaaaBBBBBBBBB	wrong side
Row 9:	Baaaaaaaaaaaaaaaaa aBBBBBBBBBaaaaaaaaa	right side
Row 8:	BBaaaaaaaaaaaaaaaaaBBBBBBBBaaaaaaaaa	wrong side
Row 7:	BBBaaaaaaaaaaaaaaaaaBBBBBBBaaaaaaaaa	right side
Row 6:	BBBBaaaaaaaaaaaaaaaaaBBBBBBaaaaaaaaa	wrong side
Row 5:	BBBBBaaaaaaaaaaaaaaaaaBBBBBaaaaaaaaa	right side
Row 4:	BBBBBBaaaaaaaaaaaaaaaaaBBBBaaaaaaaaa	wrong side
Row 3:	BBBBBBBaaaaaaaaaaaaaaaaaBBBaaaaaaaaa	right side
Row 2:	BBBBBBBBaaaaaaaaaaaaaaaaaBBaaaaaaaaa	wrong side
Row 1:	BBBBBBBBBaaaaaaaaaaaaaaaaaBaaaaaaaaa	right side
Base Chain	BBBBBBBBBBaaaaaaaaaaaaaaaaaBaaaaaaaaaA	ch 37

Square Six/Buckeye

When you see how beautifully the Buckeye motif repeats itself as an overall pattern, you'll understand why it's also called Buckeye Beauty. As you follow the pattern graph you'll see that you're once again working with Plain Patches and Double Triangles strung across a row.

Square Six/Buckeye

a = beige B = brown

Row 36:	`aaaaaaaaaaaaaaaaaBaaaaaaaaaBBBBBBBBB`	wrong side
Row 35:	`aaaaaaaaaaaaaaaaBBaaaaaaaaaBBBBBBBB`	right side
Row 34:	`aaaaaaaaaaaaaaaBBBaaaaaaaaaBBBBBBBB`	wrong side
Row 33:	`aaaaaaaaaaaaaaBBBBaaaaaaaaaBBBBBBBB`	right side
Row 32:	`aaaaaaaaaaaaaBBBBBaaaaaaaaaBBBBBBBB`	wrong side
Row 31:	`aaaaaaaaaaaaBBBBBBaaaaaaaaaBBBBBBBB`	right side
Row 30:	`aaaaaaaaaaaBBBBBBBaaaaaaaaaBBBBBBBB`	wrong side
Row 29:	`aaaaaaaaaaBBBBBBBBaaaaaaaaaBBBBBBBB`	right side
Row 28:	`aaaaaaaaaBBBBBBBBBaaaaaaaaaBBBBBBBB`	wrong side
Row 27:	`aaaaaaaaBBBBBBBBBBBBBBBBBBaaaaaaaaa`	right side
Row 26:	`aaaaaaaBBBBBBBBBBBBBBBBBBBaaaaaaaaa`	wrong side
Row 25:	`aaaaaaBBBBBBBBBBBBBBBBBBBBaaaaaaaaa`	right side
Row 24:	`aaaaaBBBBBBBBBBBBBBBBBBBBBaaaaaaaaa`	wrong side
Row 23:	`aaaaBBBBBBBBBBBBBBBBBBBBBBaaaaaaaaa`	right side
Row 22:	`aaaBBBBBBBBBBBBBBBBBBBBBBBaaaaaaaaa`	wrong side
Row 21:	`aaBBBBBBBBBBBBBBBBBBBBBBBBaaaaaaaaa`	right side
Row 20:	`aBBBBBBBBBBBBBBBBBBBBBBBBBaaaaaaaaa`	wrong side
Row 19:	`BBBBBBBBBBBBBBBBBBBBBBBBBBaaaaaaaaa`	right side
Row 18:	`aaaaaaaaaBBBBBBBBBBBBBBBBBBBBBBBBBB`	wrong side
Row 17:	`aaaaaaaaaBBBBBBBBBBBBBBBBBBBBBBBBBa`	right side
Row 16:	`aaaaaaaaaBBBBBBBBBBBBBBBBBBBBBBBBaa`	wrong side
Row 15:	`aaaaaaaaaBBBBBBBBBBBBBBBBBBBBBBBaaa`	right side
Row 14:	`aaaaaaaaaBBBBBBBBBBBBBBBBBBBBBBaaaa`	wrong side
Row 13:	`aaaaaaaaaBBBBBBBBBBBBBBBBBBBBBaaaaa`	right side
Row 12:	`aaaaaaaaaBBBBBBBBBBBBBBBBBBBBaaaaaa`	wrong side
Row 11:	`aaaaaaaaaBBBBBBBBBBBBBBBBBBBaaaaaaa`	right side
Row 10:	`aaaaaaaaaBBBBBBBBBBBBBBBBBBaaaaaaaa`	wrong side
Row 9:	`BBBBBBBBBaaaaaaaaaBBBBBBBBBaaaaaaaaa`	right side
Row 8:	`BBBBBBBBBaaaaaaaaaBBBBBBBBaaaaaaaaa`	wrong side
Row 7:	`BBBBBBBBBaaaaaaaaaBBBBBBBaaaaaaaaaa`	right side
Row 6:	`BBBBBBBBBaaaaaaaaaBBBBBBaaaaaaaaaaa`	wrong side
Row 5:	`BBBBBBBBBaaaaaaaaaBBBBBaaaaaaaaaaaa`	right side
Row 4:	`BBBBBBBBBaaaaaaaaaBBBBaaaaaaaaaaaaa`	wrong side
Row 3:	`BBBBBBBBBaaaaaaaaaBBBaaaaaaaaaaaaaa`	right side
Row 2:	`BBBBBBBBBaaaaaaaaaBBaaaaaaaaaaaaaaa`	wrong side
Row 1:	`BBBBBBBBBaaaaaaaaaBaaaaaaaaaaaaaaaa`	right side
Base Chain	`BBBBBBBBBaaaaaaaaaBaaaaaaaaaaaaaaaaaA`	ch 37

Square Seven/Pinwheel

This pinwheel motif, also known as Louisiana, consists of four Triple Triangles and Plain Patch Squares, joined perpendicularly. Make and assemble it as follows:

• With beige, sc a Plain Patch segment (17 sc, 8 rows—switch to rust on last yo), cont with a Triple Triangle (9 rows—beg with 8 rust, 1 brown, 8 rust).

• *Sc a Triple Triangle along the beige-rust side of the patch just completed (beg at the base of the center triangle (1 rust, 15 brown, 1 rust). When you complete the Triple Triangle, switch to beige for a Plain Patch as in step 1. Rep from * 2×.

• Sew join the seam between the first and last units.

Square Eight Pinwheel 4-Patch

Another pinwheel, this one made with 4 Double Triangle Squares (Row-by-Row Patch Seven) worked two at a time (See pattern graph for detailed instructions) and alternated with a 4-Patch Checkerboard Grid Square (Row-by-Row Patch Five).

a = beige B = brown

Row 36:	BBBBBBBBBaaaaaaaaaaaaaaaaaaBBBBBBBBB	wrong side
Row 35:	BBBBBBBBBaaaaaaaaaBaaaaaaaaaBBBBBBBBBa	right side
Row 34:	BBBBBBBBBaaaaaaaaaBBaaaaaaaaBBBBBBBaa	wrong side
Row 33:	BBBBBBBBBaaaaaaaaaBBBaaaaaaaBBBBBBaaa	right side
Row 32:	BBBBBBBBBaaaaaaaaaBBBBaaaaaBBBBBaaaa	wrong side
Row 31:	BBBBBBBBBaaaaaaaaaBBBBBaaaaBBBaaaaaa	right side
Row 30:	BBBBBBBBBaaaaaaaaaBBBBBaaaBBBaaaaaa	wrong side
Row 29:	BBBBBBBBBaaaaaaaaaBBBBBBaaBBaaaaaaa	right side
Row 28:	BBBBBBBBBaaaaaaaaaBBBBBBBaBaaaaaaaa	wrong side
Row 27:	aaaaaaaaaBBBBBBBBBaaaaaaaaBBBBBBBBBB	right side
Row 26:	aaaaaaaaaBBBBBBBBBaaaaaaaBBaBBBBBBBB	wrong side
Row 25:	aaaaaaaaaBBBBBBBBBaaaaaaBBBaaBBBBBBB	right side
Row 24:	aaaaaaaaaBBBBBBBBBaaaaaBBBBaaaBBBBBB	wrong side
Row 23:	aaaaaaaaaBBBBBBBBBaaaaBBBBBaaaaBBBBB	right side
Row 22:	aaaaaaaaaBBBBBBBBBaaaBBBBBBaaaaaBBBB	wrong side
Row 21:	aaaaaaaaaBBBBBBBBBaaBBBBBBBaaaaaaBBB	right side
Row 20:	aaaaaaaaaBBBBBBBBBaBBBBBBBBaaaaaaaBB	wrong side
Row 19:	aaaaaaaaaBBBBBBBBBBBBBBBBBBaaaaaaaaB	right side
Row 18:	BBBBBBBBBaaaaaaaaaBaaaaaaaaaBBBBBBBBB	wrong side
Row 17:	aBBBBBBBBaaaaaaaaaBaaaaaaaaaBBBBBBBBB	right side
Row 16:	aaBBBBBBBaaaaaaaaBBaaaaaaaaaBBBBBBBBB	wrong side
Row 15:	aaaBBBBBBaaaaaaaBBBaaaaaaaaaBBBBBBBBB	right side
Row 14:	aaaaBBBBBaaaaaBBBBaaaaaaaaaaBBBBBBBBB	wrong side
Row 13:	aaaaaBBBBaaaaBBBBBaaaaaaaaaaBBBBBBBBB	right side
Row 12:	aaaaaaBBBaaaBBBBBBaaaaaaaaaaBBBBBBBBB	wrong side
Row 11:	aaaaaaaBBaaBBBBBBBaaaaaaaaaaBBBBBBBBB	right side
Row 10:	aaaaaaaaBaBBBBBBBBaaaaaaaaaaBBBBBBBBB	wrong side
Row 9:	BBBBBBBBBBaaaaaaaaBBBBBBBBBBaaaaaaaaa	right side
Row 8:	BBBBBBBBaBBaaaaaaaaBBBBBBBBBBaaaaaaaaa	wrong side
Row 7:	BBBBBBBaaBBaaaaaaaaBBBBBBBBBBaaaaaaaaa	right side
Row 6:	BBBBBBaaaBBBaaaaaaBBBBBBBBBBaaaaaaaaa	wrong side
Row 5:	BBBBBaaaaBBBBaaaaaBBBBBBBBBBaaaaaaaaa	right side
Row 4:	BBBBaaaaaBBBBBaaaaBBBBBBBBBBaaaaaaaaa	wrong side
Row 3:	BBBaaaaaaBBBBBBaaaBBBBBBBBBBaaaaaaaaa	right side
Row 2:	BBaaaaaaaBBBBBBBaaBBBBBBBBBBaaaaaaaaa	wrong side
Row 1:	BaaaaaaaaBBBBBBBBaBBBBBBBBBBaaaaaaaaa	right side
Base Chain	aaaaaaaaaBBBBBBBBBBBBBBBBBBaaaaaaaaaA	ch 37

162

Square Nine Crosses & Losses

Crosses & Losses consists of two quilt motifs worked as 4 units, each crocheted to the side edge of the previous one as in square 7. The first motif, a large Double Triangle, begins with a Ch-18 in rust plus a turning chain in beige. Follow the pattern graph to make the second motif which combines small Double Triangles and Plain patches (the side edge to which this unit is crocheted serves as the foundation ch).

a = beige B = brown
Note: The foundation chain for this patch is the side edge of the Double Triangle

Row 18:	aaaaaaaaaaaaaaaaaa	wrong side
Row 17:	aaaaaaaaaBaaaaaaaa	right side
Row 16:	aaaaaaaaaBBaaaaaaa	wrong side
Row 15:	aaaaaaaaaBBBaaaaaa	right side
Row 14:	aaaaaaaaaBBBBaaaaa	wrong side
Row 13:	aaaaaaaaaBBBBBaaaa	right side
Row 12:	aaaaaaaaaBBBBBBaaa	wrong side
Row 11:	aaaaaaaaaBBBBBBBaa	right side
Row 10:	aaaaaaaaaBBBBBBBBa	wrong side
Row 9:	BBBBBBBBBaaaaaaaaa	right side
Row 8:	aBBBBBBBBaaaaaaaaB	wrong side
Row 7:	aaBBBBBBBaaaaaaaaB	right side
Row 6:	aaaBBBBBBaaaaaaaaB	wrong side
Row 5:	aaaaBBBBBaaaaaaaaB	right side
Row 4:	aaaaaBBBBaaaaaaaaa	wrong side
Row 3:	aaaaaaBBBaaaaaaaaa	right side
Row 2:	aaaaaaaBBaaaaaaaaa	wrong side
Row 1:	aaaaaaaaBaaaaaaaaa A	right side

Square Ten/Flying Dutchman

Flying Dutchman is a variation of Square 7, with 4 Double Triple Triangle units (each with 1 rust and beige and 1 brown and beige triangle). Make and assemble as follows:
• Beg the first unit at the point of a rust Triple Triangle (ch 8 beige, 1 rust, 8 beige).
• *Sc another unit to the side edge of the first, starting at the base of the brown center triangle (8 beige, 1 brown, 8 beige). Rep from * 2× and sew join the open seam.

Square Eleven Double 8-Patch

This Double Eight-Patch, like Patience Double Nine Patch, (Project #9), uses reverse shading to give one patch two different looks. See the graph pattern for how to work row-by-row. Follow the square 7 procedure to crochet unit 2 to the side edge of unit 1 and so forth (beg and end with a beige-brown Eight-Patch).

a = beige B = brown c = rust
side edge = foundation row except for first unit made

Unit One

Row 16:	aaaaBBBBBBBBBBBB	wrong side
Row 15:	aaaaBBBBBBBBBBBB	right side
Row 14:	aaaaBBBBBBBBBBBB	wrong side
Row 13:	aaaaBBBBBBBBBBBB	right side
Row 12:	BBBBBBBBaaaaBBBB	wrong side
Row 11:	BBBBBBBBaaaaBBBB	right side
Row 10:	BBBBBBBBaaaaBBBB	wrong side
Row 9:	BBBBBBBBaaaaBBBB	right side
Row 8:	BBBBaaaaBBBBBBBB	wrong side
Row 7:	BBBBaaaaBBBBBBBB	right side
Row 6:	BBBBaaaaBBBBBBBB	wrong side
Row 5:	BBBBaaaaBBBBBBBB	right side
Row 4:	BBBBBBBBBBBBaaaa	wrong side
Row 3:	BBBBBBBBBBBBaaaa	right side
Row 2:	BBBBBBBBBBBBaaaa	wrong side
Row 1:	BBBBBBBBBBBBaaaa	right side
Base Chain	BBBBBBBBBBBBaaaaA	ch 17

Unit Two

Beige/Brown/rust

Row 16:	aaaaaaaaaaaaBBBB	wrong
Row 15:	aaaaaaaaaaaaBBBB	right
Row 14:	aaaaaaaaaaaaBBBB	wrong
Row 13:	aaaaaaaaaaaaBBBB	right
Row 12:	aaaaccccaaaaaaaa	wrong
Row 11:	aaaaccccaaaaaaaa	right
Row 10:	aaaaccccaaaaaaaa	wrong
Row 9:	aaaaccccaaaaaaaa	right
Row 8:	aaaaaaaaccccaaaa	wrong
Row 7:	aaaaaaaaccccaaaa	right
Row 6:	aaaaaaaaccccaaaa	wrong
Row 5:	aaaaaaaaccccaaaa	right
Row 4:	BBBBaaaaaaaaaaaa	wrong
Row 3:	BBBBaaaaaaaaaaaa	right
Row 2:	BBBBaaaaaaaaaaaa	wrong
Row 1:	BBBBaaaaaaaaaaaaA	right

Square Twelve/Graphed Octagon and Checkerboard Grid

The graphed Octagon (Patch Seventeen) and Checkerboard Grid (Row-by-Row Patch Five) team up in a pattern that would be even more striking if repeated for an entire afghan. Both patches beg with a ch-19 (6 brown, 6 beige, 7 brown for the Octagon, 6 rust, 6 brown, 7 rust for the Checkerboard). Follow the Square Seven procedure to crochet join the units. For a completely different look, reverse the colors.

Square Thirteen/King's Crown

King's Crown would make a nifty overall pattern when alternated with the Star. Start it with a rust Solid Center-Out Square (Chain-and-Turn method, 4¾ inch square—60 sts), add a beige Corner Triangle to each edge (sc in each of 15 sts to beg, complete in ridge st). Add the border as follows:

Round 1: *With brown, sc into each of 20 edge sts, from the point of one triangle to the next. Switch to beige on the 20th st, work 3 sc into the corner st, switch back to brown and rep from * to end of rnd. End rnd with a sl st join to the first sc. Ch 1 now and throughout.

Round 2: In first rnd color pattern, sc in each sc (switch to beige on 20th st of each side (1 sc in next sc, 3 sc in next sc, 1 sc in next sc), sl st in first sc.

Round 3: Rep rnd 2 (sc in each of 2 sc after 20th st, 3 sc into next sc, 2 sc in next sc).

Round 4: *With beige, sc in each of the 20 brown sc along the side of the square (work corners in brown/beige brown color sequence—1 sc in each of 3 sc, 3 sc in next sc, 1 sc in each of 3 sc).

Round 5: Rep rnd 4. At corner, sc into each brown sc in brown (work beige corner with 1 sc in each of 2 sc, 3 sc in next sc, 1 sc in each of next sc), sc in each brown sc in brown.

Round 6: Rep Rnd 5 (work beige corner with 1 sc in each of 3 sc in next sc, 1 sc in each of next 3 sc).

Square Fourteen/Star

This is a single crochet version of the Star in project #26. If you make the Center-Out Square in the same color as the Fill-In Squares, the Star will have a completely different look when pieced into an all-over pattern. To make it, sc a brown Center-Out Square using the Chain-and-Turn method (5 inches square—76 sts all around). Next, sc a brown and beige Triple Triangle to each side (beg with 9 brown, 1 beige, 9 brown). Finally, sc a beige Fill-In Square into each corner (beg with 8 sts into each edge).

Square Fifteen/Fair and Square

Fair and Square, like King's Crown, would produce a handsome afghan when alternated with the Star. Beg with a rust Center-Out Square (Chain-and-Turn Method, 5 inches square). With beige, sc a 10-row Plain Patch to each side (17 sts per row), and fill in the corners with brown Fill-In Squares (beg with 8 sts into each edge).

General Finishing Instructions

1. *With rust, ridge st in the edge sts around each square (2 sts in sts before and after each corner), sl st in first ridge st. Ch 1. Rep from *2× (skip corner incs on middle rnd).

2. Crochet join the squares as per the assembly diagram.

3. *With rust, ridge stitch into the edge sts around the pieced sampler in a gauge decreased by a stitch for every 4 inches (2 sts in the sts before and after each corner), sl st in first ridge st. Ch 1. Rep from * 3×. Fasten off.

Supply Sources

The yarns used to make the projects in this book are available in retail yarn outlets throughout the country. Quilt batting can be bought in stores catering to hand and machine sewers and by mail. Many other fine and colorful yarns are available. If you can't locate a yarn you'd like to use, use the list below to contact the manufacturer for the name and address of the retail outlet nearest you. Yarns listed at the beginning of each project are identified by the manufacturer's name. Whenever a manufacture uses numbers instead of names to identify colors, you'll find them in parentheses next to the generic color name.

Bernat Yarn & Craft Corp.
Depot and Mendon Sts.
Uxbridge, MA 01569

Charity Hill Farm Inc.
Hardwick, MA 01037

Coats & Clark Inc.
P.O. Box 1966
Stamford, CT 06904

Fairfield Processing Corporation
(Poly-Fil brand stuffing)
P. O. Box 1157
Danbury, CT 06810

Lane Borgosesia
128 Radio Circle
Mt. Kisco, NY 10549

Lily Craft Products
B. Blumenthal & Co. Inc.
140 Kero Road
Carlstadt, NJ 07072

Nevada Yarn Company
80 13th Avenue
Ronkonkoma, NY 11779

Phildar Inc.
6438 Dawson Blvd.
Norcross, GA 30093
toll free order number
(800) 241-5348

Plymouth Yarn Co.
500 Lafayette St.
Box 28
Bristol, PA 19007

Scheepjeswol USA Inc.
155 Lafayette Ave.
White Plains, NY 10603

Talon American
High Bridge Park
P. O. Box 3823
Stamford, CT 08905

William Unger & Co.
230 Fifth Avenue
New York, NY 10001

Index